The Homestead Strike

On July 6, 1892, three hundred armed Pinkerton agents arrived by boat in Homestead, Pennsylvania to retake the Carnegie Steelworks from the company's striking workers. As the agents tried to disembark, shots rang out and a violent skirmish began. The confrontation at Homestead was a turning point in the history of American unionism, beginning a rapid process of decline for America's steel unions that lasted until the Great Depression.

Examining the strike's origins, events, and legacy, *The Homestead Strike* illuminates the tense relationship between labor, capital, and government in the pivotal moment between Reconstruction and the Progressive Era. In a concise narrative, bolstered by statements from steelworkers, court testimony, and excerpts from Carnegie's writings, Paul Kahan introduces students to one of the most dramatic and influential episodes in the history of American labor.

Paul Kahan teaches history at Ohlone College in Fremont, California. For more information, visit his website at www.paulkahan.com.

Critical Moments in American History
Edited by *William Thomas Allison*

The Battle of the Greasy Grass/Little Bighorn
Custer's Last Stand in Memory, History, and Popular Culture
Debra Buchholtz

The Assassination of John F. Kennedy
Political Trauma and American Memory
Alice L. George

Freedom to Serve
Truman, Civil Rights, and Executive Order 9981
Jon E. Taylor

The Battles of Kings Mountain and Cowpens
The American Revolution in the Southern Backcountry
Melissa Walker

The Cuban Missile Crisis
The Threshold of Nuclear War
Alice L. George

The Nativist Movement in America
Religious Conflict in the 19th Century
Katie Oxx

The 1980 Presidential Election
Ronald Reagan and the Shaping of the American Conservative Movement
Jeffrey D. Howison

The Fort Pillow Massacre
North, South, and the Status of African Americans in the Civil War Era
Bruce Tap

The Louisiana Purchase
A Global Context
Robert D. Bush

From Selma to Montgomery
The Long March to Freedom
Barbara Harris Combs

The Homestead Strike
Labor, Violence, and American Industry
Paul Kahan

The Homestead Strike

Labor, Violence, and American Industry

Paul Kahan

Routledge
Taylor & Francis Group

NEW YORK AND LONDON

First published 2014
by Routledge
711 Third Avenue, New York, NY 10017

and by Routledge
2 Park Square, Milton Park, Abingdon, Oxon OX14 4RN

Routledge is an imprint of the Taylor & Francis Group, an informa business

Library of Congress Cataloging in Publication Data
Kahan, Paul.
   The Homestead Strike: labor, violence, and American industry/
   Paul E. Kahan.
   pages cm.—(Critical moments in American history)
   Includes bibliographical references.
   1. Homestead Strike, Homestead, Pa., 1892.   2. Carnegie, Andrew,
   1835–1919.   3. Carnegie Steel Company—History.   4. Steel industry
   and trade—Pennsylvania—History—19th century.   5. Iron and steel
   workers—Pennsylvania—History—19th century.   6. Working class—
   Pennsylvania—History—19th century.   I. Title.
   HD5325.I51892 .K34 2013
   331.892′8691420974885—dc23
   2013026208

ISBN: 978-0-415-53193-1 (hbk)
ISBN: 978-0-415-53194-8 (pbk)
ISBN: 978-0-203-08147-1 (ebk)

Typeset in Bembo and Helvetica Neue
by Florence Production Ltd, Stoodleigh, Devon, UK

Printed and bound in the United States of America by Publishers Graphics,
LLC on sustainably sourced paper.

Contents

Series Introduction

Welcome to the Routledge *Critical Moments in American History* series. The purpose of this new series is to give students a window into the historian's craft through concise, readable books by leading scholars, who bring together the best scholarship and engaging primary sources to explore a critical moment in the American past. In discovering the principal points of the story in these books, gaining a sense of historiography, following a fresh trail of primary documents, and exploring suggested readings, students can then set out on their own journey, to debate the ideas presented, interpret primary sources, and reach their own conclusions—just like the historian.

A critical moment in history can be a range of things—a pivotal year, the pinnacle of a movement or trend, or an important event such as the passage of a piece of legislation, an election, a court decision, a battle. It can be social, cultural, political, or economic. It can be heroic or tragic. Whatever they are, such moments are by definition "game changers," momentous changes in the pattern of the American fabric, paradigm shifts in the American experience. Many of the critical moments explored in this series are familiar; some less so.

There is no ultimate list of critical moments in American history—any group of students, historians, or other scholars may come up with a different catalog of topics. These differences of view, however, are what make history itself and the study of history so important and so fascinating. Therein can be found the utility of historical inquiry—to explore, to challenge, to understand, and to realize the legacy of the past through its influence on the present. It is the hope of this series to help students realize this intrinsic value of our past and of studying our past.

William Thomas Allison
Georgia Southern University

Figures

Acknowledgments

Like all writers, I accrued a great many debts in writing this book. While I cannot possibly thank everyone who contributed to *The Homestead Strike: Labor, Violence, and American Industry*, there are some people who deserve recognition. First, I would like to thank Ron Baraff, Director of Museum Collections and Archives at the Rivers of Steel National Heritage Area. Ron's incomparable knowledge of Rivers of Steel's resources and his willingness to read portions of the manuscript assisted in making *Homestead* the best book possible. Similarly, I want to thank Julie Ludwig, Associate Archivist at the Frick Collection and Frick Art Reference Library. With only the vaguest of instructions, Julie was able to track down the perfect image for inclusion in Homestead. People such as Ron and Julie make books such as *The Homestead Strike* possible!

In addition, I want to thank my wife Jennifer and my son Alec, both of whom willingly "picked up the slack" around the house so that I could finish writing this book. Amazingly, my wife was willing to do so despite being pregnant; our daughter, Zoe Kahan, was born while I was in the midst of revising the manuscript. I dedicate *The Homestead Strike: Labor, Violence, and American Industry* to all of them.

Timeline

1835: November 25	Andrew Carnegie is born.
1848: May	Carnegie and his family migrate to the United States.
1849: December 19	Henry Clary Frick is born.
1885: January 2	The *New York Times* dubs Carnegie the "Millionaire Socialist."
1886: April	The first of Carnegie's articles endorsing the right of workers to unionize appears in *Forum*. A second article appears in the same publication four months later.
1889: July	Carnegie and Frick settle a strike and lockout at the Homestead works by signing a three-year contract that recognizes the workers' right to collective bargaining.
1892: June	Frick offers the union a "take it or leave it" contract, setting a deadline of June 24, and then refuses to negotiate. The union rejects his offer.
1892: June 25	Frick orders notices posted at Homestead that the company will no longer deal with the union, only individual workers. That same day, he contacts the Pinkerton National Detective Agency to arrange for private guards ("Pinkertons") to be dispatched to Homestead to guard the company's property.
1892: June 29	Frick begins shutting down various departments at Homestead, a process completed the following day, at which point the workers are locked out.
1892: July 6	The Pinkerton agents try to take control of the closed Homestead works; hours of bloody fighting ensue, and the striking workers and townspeople prevent the Pinkertons from entering the works.
1892: July 12	The Pennsylvania state militia arrives in the town to restore order and return the works to Carnegie Steel. They remain until October 13.
1892: July 23	In an attempt to aid the strikers, an anarchist named Alexander Berkman tries to assassinate Henry Clay Frick. Frick survives the attempt and Berkman is sentenced to 22 years in Western State Penitentiary.
1892: November 20	Economic necessity forces the workers to return to work, and they vote to end the strike.

Introduction

In the early morning hours of July 6, 1892, a tugboat pulling two barges slowly crept up the Ohio River toward Homestead, a steel town just outside Pittsburgh, Pennsylvania. Inside the barges, approximately 300 agents of the infamous Pinkerton National Detective Agency nervously clutched their Winchester rifles; their goal was to retake the Carnegie Steel Works from the company's striking workers, who had occupied the site a few days earlier. As they approached the town, the Pinkerton men could see that a group of striking steel workers armed with sticks, stones, and guns had gathered at the town's wharf. The battle that followed is one of the most infamous and critical moments in American labor history.

One of the participants called it a massive conspiracy hatched by big business and aided by the government to deprive workers of their rights. Andrew Carnegie called it (inaccurately) the one serious quarrel between himself and his workers during all his years in business. Yet, this explosion of violence outside of Pittsburgh in July 1892 often rates only a few sentences in many U.S. history textbooks, if it is mentioned at all. Today's students can be forgiven, therefore, if they are unaware of the terrible events that shook Western Pennsylvania. Regardless, the events that unfolded in this small Pennsylvanian town shed light on many of our contemporary concerns about politics, economics, and labor.

Too often, we think of historical events as just that—discrete episodes pulled from the larger story of American history. I hope that *The Homestead Strike: Labor, Violence, and American Industry* challenges that understanding. A large portion of this book is devoted to the background of the Homestead Strike so that readers understand not only *what* happened, but *why*. The events at Homestead resulted from a combination of large economic, political, and social changes, as well as specific decisions made by the individual participants (mostly, but not exclusively, Andrew Carnegie and

Henry Clay Frick). Therefore, the Homestead Strike is a good illustration of two key historical concepts: agency and context. Agency simply refers to a person's ability to do something or to make a choice, and it is important because we experience history backward: we know how the story ends because it has already happened. Looking backward, it might seem to us that there are no choices, that the events at Homestead unfolded the way they were "supposed to." This is the opposite of agency and is very different from how events look in the present, where people face many choices whose outcomes are uncertain. My hope is that, after reading *The Homestead Strike*, you will understand historic events as the people who lived through them did: as uncertain and contingent on the decisions made in the moment. At any one of a hundred points, a different decision could have changed the strike's outcome.

Of course, agency is not limitless—there are economic, social, and legal limits on the available choices. For instance, you are constrained in your choice of cars and houses by how much money you have (or can borrow), so you may have to settle for a Toyota instead of the Lamborghini you really want. This brings us to a second important concept: context. If agency means that people are free to make their own decisions, context limits the available possibilities and makes certain outcomes more likely than others. All historical events take place in a specific historical context that helps shape their outcome by limiting the individual actors' range of choices. Homestead is a great illustration of the intersection between agency and context in shaping crucial events in American history.

The first chapter explores the two most important people associated with the Homestead Strike: Andrew Carnegie and Henry Clay Frick. It was their decisions, more than anyone else's, that set in motion the events at Homestead and determined the strike's outcome. While most readers are undoubtedly familiar with Andrew Carnegie, fewer are likely to recognize Henry Clay Frick. Yet, in their time, these men were both incredibly well known as two of the most important industrialists of their time. Their partnership created one of the most profitable and largest corporations in American history but also led to the tragic events at Homestead. It is impossible to understand these events without first understanding Carnegie and Frick as individuals and as "captains of industry."

The second chapter explores the larger economic and political context in which Carnegie and Frick lived. The last three decades of the nineteenth century saw a dramatic shift in the size and scope of American companies, which increased the distance between owners and their employers and led to more frequent (and more violent) confrontations. One consequence was the growth of labor unionism, which resulted in more frequent confrontations between employers and their employees that sometimes turned violent.

The third chapter moves from the general to the specific, exploring Carnegie and Frick's approach to dealing with their workers in this changed circumstance and chronicles the almost consistent tension between them and their workers in the years leading up to Homestead. Frick and Carnegie actively and aggressively worked to break the unions in their steel plants and coalfields in the 1880s, creating a pattern that would be repeated at Homestead.

The fourth chapter provides a detailed narrative history of the strike itself. It explores a number of themes, including the cozy relationship between big business and government at the end of the nineteenth century. Using an array of sources, *The Homestead Strike* provides one of the most detailed narrative histories of this overlooked but crucial turning point in American labor history.

The fourth and fifth chapters examine the Homestead Strike, its immediate aftermath, and its legacy, illustrating the long-lasting effects of the explosive collision between workers and the profit imperative. As these chapters make clear, though the strikers succeeded in winning the battle, a series of unpredictable events (including a slapdash assassination attempt!) cost the Amalgamated Association of Iron and Steel Workers (AAISW) the war. Homestead, which looked to be a moment of triumph for labor unionism in the steel industry, actually signaled its death knell, and by the end of the nineteenth century, the AAISW (which had once been one of the most powerful unions in the United States) had all but disappeared from America's steel mills.

Throughout the book, I use the terms *lockout* and *strike* to describe what happened at Homestead. A strike is a body of employees' organized refusal to work, usually undertaken to force a concession from the employer. A lockout, by contrast, is when an employer prevents employees from working by denying them access to the workplace (i.e., locking them out). The events at Homestead were both a lockout (because Frick shut down the Homestead works and thereby prevented his employees from working) and a strike (because the AAISW voted to strike to force the company to negotiate over wages). For simplicity, I most often refer to the events at Homestead as a strike because this reflects general usage (i.e., most people call what happened at Homestead the "Homestead Strike"). In addition, I use the word *scab* to refer to replacement workers imported by management to break a strike. This is mostly due to space considerations—"replacement workers brought in to end the strike" is a cumbersome phrase, and readers would likely tire of reading it. While some might argue that the use of the term *scab* implies a value judgment about these workers, none is intended.

It is important to note that the battles over wealth inequality, working conditions, and the rights of workers to collectively bargain will seem eerily familiar, which is one of the book's central themes. Although contemporary events inspired me to write *The Homestead Strike*, I do not believe that "history repeats itself," despite the multiple student papers I receive each semester that argue otherwise. Perhaps the better argument comes from Mark Twain, who wrote, "History does not repeat itself, but it does rhyme."

CHAPTER 1

Carnegie and Frick

The two most important individuals involved in the Homestead Strike were undoubtedly Andrew Carnegie and Henry Clay Frick. It was these two individuals, more than anyone else, who set in motion the tragic events at Homestead. To fully comprehend what happened at Homestead, it is essential to understand a few things about both Carnegie and Frick. The first is that while both saw themselves as "self-made men," or individuals who achieved great wealth and power through nothing but their own intelligence and hard work, the truth is more complicated. Both Frick and Carnegie got their start using money and connections provided by their families or mentors. Both men consistently resorted to questionable tactics and unethical behavior to ensure high rates of return on their investments. Once established, they organized or joined industry organizations and supported special interest legislation that effectively prevented new competitors from competing with their businesses, effectively stymieing other would-be "self-made men."

Andrew Carnegie was born in Dunfermline, Scotland, on November 25, 1835, to William and Margaret Carnegie. William Carnegie was a weaver who worked out of the family's house, and he was a Chartist, supporting a political philosophy that advocated universal male suffrage and annual parliamentary elections, demands that were radical for the time. William was not the only radical in Andrew's family; Margaret's father could always be counted on to appear at local town meetings and heckle his conservative political opponents. Her brother, Tom Morrison, pressed the workers of Dunfermline to walk off the job in solidarity with the miners in nearby Clackmannan County after the latter went out on strike.[1] During the 1840s, Carnegie's father and uncles led strikes as technological advances and worsening economic conditions made providing for their families impossible. In other words, from a very young age, Andrew

Figure 1.1 Henry Clay Frick (left) and Andrew Carnegie (right) were two of
America's leading industrialists and the two men most responsible for
the violence at Homestead in July 1892.
Courtesy of The Frick Collection/Frick Art Reference Library Archives.

Carnegie was continually exposed to a radical, pro-labor politics that was
at great variance with the actions he later took as an adult.

One reason for their radicalism was the fact that the late 1840s were
lean times in Scotland. Called the "Hungry Forties," work for men such
as William evaporated; between 1840 and 1850, the number of handloom
weavers declined from approximately 85,000 to about 25,000 a drop of
almost 70 percent. The massive unemployment sparked food riots all over
Scotland, and the Carnegie family's modest circumstances worsened.[2]
Margaret was forced to sell vegetables and sweetmeats or take in piecework
to supplement the family's meager income. As a result, William Carnegie
decided to move his family to the United States, but poverty forced him
to accept a loan from one of Margaret's childhood friends in order to
purchase the tickets. In May 1848, when Andrew was 13, the Carnegies
crossed the Atlantic and began their lives in the "New World."

The Carnegies settled in Allegheny County, where Margaret's
sisters lived. Like many recent immigrants, the Carnegies were poor; the

name of their neighborhood—Barefoot Square—was a testament to the deprivations they suffered. William initially tried to manufacture and sell his weaving, but he was unable to compete with the cheap, mass-produced goods pouring out of America's expanding factories. Worse, William's income did not meet the family's needs, so Margaret again took in piecework binding shoes. Eventually, her income exceeded William's, which only demoralized the proud Scot. Years later, Andrew reflected on these events and, implicitly blaming his father for being unable to adapt to the changing economic climate, said, "My father did not recognize the impending revolution and was struggling under the old system."[3]

Andrew Carnegie first worked in a factory that manufactured bobbins (cylinders on which yarn, thread, or wire is wound), where he was paid $1.20 for a 72-hour week. It was not long before factory owner, John Hay, approached Carnegie to draft some letters; apparently, Hay had poor handwriting and was so impressed with Carnegie's penmanship that he paid the teenager to draft the invoices sent to the factory's customers. Seeing an opportunity, Carnegie took evening classes in accounting during the winter of 1849 and used what he learned to increase his skills (and income). That spring, Carnegie's uncle found the boy a position as a messenger for the Ohio Telegraph Company, which paid more than double what Carnegie had earned in the bobbin factory. This was the first instance of a family member or well-placed acquaintance securing a lucrative position or investment opportunity for Carnegie, and it became an essential ingredient in his early success.

Carnegie was soon promoted to telegraph operator and, by 18, was working for the Pennsylvania Railroad Company's manager (and future president), Thomas A. Scott, as secretary/telegraph operator.

In this position, Carnegie wielded considerable power, often acting in his boss' name without Scott's prior approval. Fortunately, Carnegie's brash behavior almost always worked out well for him, a fact that quickly endeared him to Scott. This early success reinforced his belief that he was smarter than many of his contemporaries, a feeling that, by middle age, hardened into arrogance and contributed to an implicit belief that the rules did not apply to him.

Soon, Scott was including Carnegie in his investments (the first of which Carnegie financed with a loan from Scott), and by 1858, Carnegie was earning an annual dividend of $5,000 per year.[4] Success bred more success as Carnegie consistently reinvested his gains into railroad-related industries. In the spring of 1861, Scott (who was now serving as Assistant Secretary of War) appointed the 26-year-old Carnegie as superintendent of the military railways and the federal government's eastern telegraph lines, a lucrative position that gave Carnegie multiple opportunities to increase

Thomas A. Scott (1823–1881)

Thomas Alexander Scott was a wealthy and politically influential industrialist. Scott was born in Fort Loudoun, a small town in Central Pennsylvania. In 1850, he accepted a position as a station agent with the Pennsylvania Railroad and rose quickly through the company's ranks; within a decade, he was the company's vice president. Briefly serving as the Union Pacific Railroad's president in the early 1870s, Scott became president of the Pennsylvania Railroad in 1874 and was largely responsible for its growth into one of the nation's leading railroads.

Scott's wealth and power made him influential in the state's nascent Republican Party. In the early months of the Civil War, Pennsylvania's first Republican governor, Andrew G. Curtin (1861–1867) commissioned Scott a colonel and, shortly thereafter, Abraham Lincoln appointed Scott Assistant Secretary of War. Drawing on his professional experience, Scott eventually coordinated and supervised the federal government's railroads. Following the war, Scott played a prominent role in Reconstruction, the federal government's process of readmitting the former Confederate states back into the Union.

his personal wealth. In other words, Carnegie's early success had far more to do with being in the right place at the right time than in any personal qualities.

In large measure, Scott's success was due to the fact that he was aggressive, ruthless, manipulative, and willing to operate in ethical gray areas in search of greater profit. For instance, Scott and Pennsylvania Railroad president J. Edgar Thomson participated in a price-fixing cartel with the managements of Baltimore and Ohio Railroad and Ohio and Mississippi Railroad (among others) that ensured fat profits by limiting competition. Scott manipulated the media by promising newspapers additional advertising in exchange for favorable coverage, and he was not above offering influential journalists and government officials "gifts" in exchange for favorable treatment. During the Civil War, Congress investigated Scott for price-gouging the government; the investigation turned up evidence that Scott favored the Pennsylvania Railroad when it came to directing federal government rail traffic in order to raise the company's profits. All of these were methods that Carnegie later employed in building his steel empire.

Another method of ensuring a healthy bottom line was for Thomson, Scott, and Carnegie to invest their private money in an idea or product for which their other businesses (in this case, the Pennsylvania Railroad) would be an enthusiastic customer. One good example was Theodore T.

Woodruff's improved design for sleeping cars, a train car whose seats could be converted into beds so that passengers could sleep during long trips. In the late 1850s, Thomson and Scott ordered four of Woodruff's sleeping cars for use on the Pennsylvania Railroad. This was good news for Woodruff, but he lacked the funds to actually build the cars at the time (he had only a single demonstration model). Thomson and Scott offered capital in exchange for shares in Woodruff's company; since they had committed the Pennsylvania Railroad to buying Woodruff's sleeper cars, their investment was guaranteed to be a good one. Scott encouraged his protégé to invest in the company as well, which Carnegie did by taking a loan from a local bank. There is nothing illegal about this sort of "can't lose" investment, but it does demonstrate that Carnegie's rise to wealth had less to do with intelligence and hard work than ready access to capital and the good fortune of knowing people (such as Scott and Thomson) whose own wealth gave them the means to ensure a decent return on their investments.

However, it was in the growing demand for iron products that Carnegie saw his future success. The Civil War stimulated intense demand for military equipment (cannons, shells, armor plating, rifles, etc.) that was largely made of iron, driving up the price per ton. A self-described pacifist, Carnegie did not have to serve in the Union Army because he paid a poor Irish immigrant $850 to volunteer as a substitute; this left Carnegie free to exploit the vast opportunities for wealth created by the war. In 1864, Carnegie formed the first of multiple iron-related companies in the hopes of capitalizing on the boom, which he did; during this period, he bragged to a former coworker, "I'm rich; I'm rich," and by 1868, his business interests included bridge-building, railroads, petroleum, telegraphy, and finance, which brought him a combined return of over $56,000 per year.[5] Just as before, Carnegie kept investing his wealth into his companies, using the capital to improve technology, a hallmark of his approach to business throughout his life.

By the early 1870s, Carnegie began rethinking the sprawling and diverse nature of his empire. He decided to consolidate, or, as he later put it in his autobiography, "put all good eggs in one basket."[6] Undoubtedly, this new approach was encouraged by the fact that he, Thomas Scott, and J. Edgar Thomson (president of the Pennsylvania Railroad) were voted off the Union Pacific's board of directors under a cloud of scandal. Thus, in autumn of 1872, he formed Carnegie, McCandless & Company, establishing a steel plant just outside of Pittsburgh in Braddock's Field. The depression triggered by the Panic of 1873 caused the firm some financial difficulties, and it was reorganized in 1874 as the Edgar Thomson Steel Company, which quickly became both the country's leading rail producer and America's most technologically advanced steel mill. While many companies failed due to the depression, Carnegie's firm continued to expand during this period, taking advantage of cheap wages to enlarge its production facilities. Growth was slow at first, but by the late 1870s, Carnegie had elbowed his way into the influential Bessemer Steel Association, a cartel designed to ensure favorable policies and squelch competition. Using trade organizations such as this to prevent new competitors from emerging would be a preferred tactic of both Carnegie and Frick, and it helps account for their spectacular success in cornering the steel and coke markets. Carnegie's success allowed him to further consolidate his business holdings into Carnegie Brothers & Company in 1881.

By the late 1860s, however, Carnegie had largely receded from the day-to-day management of his industrial empire For instance, at about this time, Carnegie began taking extended summer trips to Europe (most often Scotland) to avoid the heat and humidity of Pittsburgh or New York. As summer neared, he would complain of the heat and assert that summers in the Mid-Atlantic might cause him heat stroke.[7] In 1867, he moved from Pittsburgh to New York, which disconnected him even further from the men whose labor actually produced his wealth. Carnegie primarily engaged with the business by reviewing the company's cost sheets, which were mailed to him once a month; in turn, he sent these back to his various division managers, often with extensive notes and ideas how best to increase profits by cutting expenses. As biographer David Nasaw noted, "Labor was, for him, simply another item on his cost sheet."[8] Paradoxically, Carnegie frequently criticized industrialists who were uninvolved in the daily operations of their plants, an arrangement he called "one great source of the trouble between employers and employed."[9] The distance shielded him from the fact that his extravagant trips and palatial homes were made possible by the men who worked 12-hour shifts in steel plants where the heat was almost intolerable. Conditions in Carnegie's mills were brutal: men often worked seven days a week, 12 hours a day, or more than double today's standard 40-hour workweek. One former steelworker recalled losing 40 pounds during his first three months on the job. He described the work as a "dog's life," saying:

> Now, those men work twelve hours and sleep and eat out ten more. You can see a man don't have much time for anything else. You can't see your friends, or do anything but work [. . .] I used to come home so exhausted, staggering.[10]

Industrial accidents were routine and claimed the lives of 15 or 20 workers in each mill annually.[11] However, distance from his works provided Carnegie with something he greatly valued: plausible deniability. If a labor dispute blew up into a violent confrontation, Carnegie could claim that it was his managers, rather than he, who were responsible, protecting his public image as a "friend of labor."

Distance from his men only contributed to another of his defects: his callousness toward other people's suffering. During the depression of 1873, when unemployment hovered at about 25 percent, Carnegie actually complained to a friend that he had to step over the homeless to get into his New York office every day.[12] When asked for loans or other types of financial assistance, Carnegie usually refused, even if the requestor was a close personal friend. For instance, in the early 1870s, Carnegie's former mentor, Thomas Scott (the man who was most responsible for Carnegie's rise to wealth), ran into severe financial difficulties and asked Carnegie for a loan. The depression had shrunk railroad traffic, hitting Scott's Texas and Pacific Railroad hard. The railroad needed to make an interest payment on an outstanding loan to avoid falling into bankruptcy, and Scott did not have the cash. Scott desperately arranged a $300,000 loan from Morgan & Company to cover the interest payment and operating expenses, but Morgan required that Carnegie assist with the financing. Scott wrote to Carnegie to secure the younger man's help, confident that the Scot would be willing to help out his former mentor. When Carnegie did not reply, Scott asked J. Edgar Thomson (who also stood to lose a considerable amount of money if the Texas and Pacific collapsed) to contact Carnegie and ask for the loan; Thomson did so and was shocked when Carnegie refused, citing that he had no money to lend given the number of people already dependent on him. Both Scott and Thomson were appalled by what they perceived as Carnegie's betrayal, but as biographer Peter Krass noted, "old loyalties certainly weren't going to hinder Carnegie's own success."[13]

Callousness was hardly Carnegie's worst fault; he was a brazen manipulator who was not above lying to increase profits. Charles Grosvenor, a congressman from Ohio and a contemporary of Carnegie's, called the steel titan "the arch-sneak of this age." Carnegie's biographers have been more nuanced: Raymond Lamont-Brown called Carnegie "a skilled manipulator," while Peter Krass asserted that he "excelled at manipulating the system."[14] In one particularly well-known episode from 1890, Carnegie's company started a rumor that the rival Duquesne Steel Company's rails were inferior. Up to this time, rail manufacturers first produced giant ingots of steel that were then melted into steel bars (called "blooms"), which were in turn reheated and shaped into rails. The Allegheny Bessemer Steel Company, which owned a mill in Duquesne, pioneered the practice of rolling ingots directly into rails (i.e., without shaping them into blooms and then reheating

Bessemer Steelmaking

The Bessemer process is an inexpensive method for mass-producing steel. Specifically, the process involves blowing oxygen on molten pig iron (iron ore that has been purified through smelting). The goal is to reduce the carbon content because pig iron's high carbon content makes the metal brittle. By oxidizing the pig iron, the carbon content declines and the iron is transformed into the more malleable (when molten) and much stronger (when cooled) steel. Another advantage was that a Bessemer mill could produce nearly 10 times more tons of steel rails per year than mills producing iron rails.

Introducing oxygen to molten pig iron during the smelting process as a way of producing steel had been practiced outside Europe for centuries, but never on a scale that would allow for the mass production of steel. In the early 1850s, two English inventors—William Kelly and Henry Bessemer—each developed methods for oxidizing pig iron that could be practiced on a large scale. Because Bessemer took out a patent on the process in 1855, his was the name attached to the process.

The Bessemer process took place in a giant pear-shaped vessel called the Bessemer converter. The converter, which was approximately 15 feet tall and mounted on two legs, had a hole at the top into which the raw elements could be mixed during the smelting process. Naturally, the converter's shape concentrated the gases and heat given off by the process, so the converter spewed sparks, flame, and even droplets of molten metal while in operation. The process itself required vast amounts of coke to operate the converter, which immediately raised demand and spurred a coke boom in the counties surrounding Pittsburgh.

With the introduction of the Bessemer process into the United States in the mid 1860s, rail production skyrocketed as the average number of tons produced annually by America's mills increased 17-fold. During the last three decades of the nineteenth century, 90 percent of American-produced Bessemer steel was processed into train rails, and almost every rail produced during this time was made of Bessemer steel. Not surprisingly, the jump in rail production pushed down prices, which fell 66 percent between 1873 and 1878. Unfortunately, Bessemer steel had few other uses; the manufacturing process produced steel that was often unreliable, so Bessemer steel could not be used for buildings or bridges and subways (these were made of open-hearth steel, an alternative manufacturing process).

In addition, the Bessemer process decisively changed workers' routines and thus required more of them. Iron puddlers worked in two-man teams and exercised a great deal of control over their furnaces and work schedules (which averaged five and one-half 12-hour days), so they could take breaks as needed. Bessemer furnaces, by contrast, operated 24 hours a day (due to the costs of and risk of damage inherent in cooling them), and the men who operated them worked full 12-hour shifts (no breaks) seven days a week. In addition, Bessemer furnace men exercised little control over their furnaces.

them); this was a labor- and time-saving innovation that meant the company could potentially produce rails more cheaply than Carnegie.

Carnegie initially moved to ban the company from the rail pool, which limited their customers to smaller, low-profit orders. Then, rather cleverly, he turned the Allegheny Bessemer Steel Company's advantage to a disadvantage by implying that failing to reheat the ingots before conversion to rails damaged the rails' "homogeneity," a rumor that biographer Harold C. Livesay called "worse than false" because it was "totally meaningless."[15] Nonetheless, the rumor frightened customers, who fretted about a defect that they did not understand. Carnegie went so far as to include a special note on the company's letterhead beginning in the autumn of 1890: "To guard against danger of flaws and ensure uniform quality, all rails are reheated and re-rolled from the bloom."[16] By November 1890, Carnegie had scooped up the Allegheny Bessemer Steel Company for a bargain, and though the Duquesne mill continued producing ingots into rails without reheating, nothing more was heard of the purported "dangers" of this practice.

Perhaps Carnegie's greatest flaw was his legendary vanity. Carnegie worried a great deal about his public image. He was a vain and pretentious man who craved the respect and admiration of those who were better educated than he to validate his inflated self-image. His nickname within the steel industry was "the Great Egoist," and one biographer called Carnegie's vanity his "Achilles heel."[17] During the 1880s, he either purchased outright or acquired a controlling share of many English newspapers, which he used as vehicles for expressing his political, social, and literary ideas. He was not shy about broadcasting his achievements: referring to William Vanderbilt (at the time, the richest man in the world), Carnegie once sniffed, "I would not exchange his millions for my knowledge of Shakespeare."[18] A self-educated man, Carnegie used his leisure to associate with some of America and Europe's best known men of letters, including Mark Twain, Matthew Arnold, and Herbert Spencer.[19] As early as 1868, Carnegie wrote a note to himself detailing his intention to retire from business and settle in Oxford so that he could purchase a newspaper and cultivate relationships with "literary men."[20] Though it would be more than a quarter century before Carnegie actually retired from business, he did begin taking extended vacations to Europe each year, and starting in the early 1880s, he published travelogues such as *An American Four-in-Hand in Britain* and *Round the World*, as well as serious economic and sociological analyses such as *Triumphant Democracy* and *The Gospel of Wealth*.

Carnegie was so concerned about his public image that, in the aftermath of the Homestead Strike, he mused about paying newspapers not to print negative stories about him or his company, a move that biographer Peter Krass compared to something a totalitarian regime might do to retain power.[21] This was surely an extreme example of Carnegie's vanity; a more representative example appeared in his autobiography, where he grossly exaggerated his role in developing the sleeping car. He asserted that he "discovered" the heretofore-unknown inventor Theodore T. Woodruff (who was unflatteringly portrayed as naive) and took Woodruff's model of a sleeping car to Pennsylvania Railroad president J. Edgar Thomson, who (along with Carnegie and Scott) invested in the idea. In reality, there were sleeping cars before Woodruff had developed his cleaner and more comfortable model, and he had sold similar systems to other railroads before contacting the Pennsylvania Railroad.[22] Worse, Carnegie had the gall to send Woodruff a signed copy of the book. Woodruff was so incensed by the inaccurate and condescending portrayal of these events that he responded with a letter criticizing Carnegie's arrogance for writing a book that was "misleading and so far from the true facts of the case." Carnegie disingenuously (and arrogantly) responded that his autobiography was not a history of sleeping cars, but "a history of the country as a whole" and therefore he could not trifle with mere details, an attitude that he expressed whenever caught in a lie.[23] It should come as no surprise that James H. Bridge, one of Carnegie Steel's earliest historians and someone who knew Andrew Carnegie personally, observed that, of all the sources he used, "[. . .] Andrew Carnegie's own narrative [was] the least trustworthy."[24] Certainly, the way that Carnegie remembered the events at Homestead bore little resemblance to what actually happened, as will become clear.

In addition to being careless with the truth, Carnegie could be extremely hypocritical. A good illustration is his decision to manufacture armor for the U.S. Navy despite being an avowed pacifist. In his 1886 book *Triumphant Democracy*, he had celebrated the United States' alleged disinterest in imperial expansion, noting proudly (if somewhat inaccurately) that the country "[. . .] has nothing worthy to rank as a ship of war."[25] In a letter to Secretary of War William Whitney, Carnegie engaged in a peculiar form of duplicity that would reappear later leading up to Homestead. Carnegie wrote:

My feeling is that if Carnegie Bros. and Co. cannot earn a living by making instruments of peace, they will conclude to starve, rather than make those of war. *But of course I will not override the voice of all my partners if they conclude otherwise, even although I hold a majority of the stock.*[26]

Carnegie's statement was, of course, totally disingenuous. As he noted in the letter, he was the majority stockholder, so he could effectively prevent the company from refusing the contract. By constructing his note this way, however, he sought to give the illusion that he (despite his scruples) had been "forced" by his board and was merely acceding to a decision that was made democratically. However, his coquettishness about military contracts did not last long. Within a few years, he went so far as to begin advocating that the company bid on armaments contracts (primarily the construction of large guns placed on ships), though some on the board disagreed, and the company did not embrace the gun-making business the way that it had armor-making.[27] Nonetheless, the story indicates that, whatever Carnegie's expressed principles, when money was involved, he was first and foremost a capitalist.

One key aspect of Carnegie's public image that he zealously guarded was his reputation for being a "friend of labor." As the next chapter makes clear, this reputation had more to do with what he said than what he actually did, but it is clear that *he* thought himself a friend of labor and worked hard to cultivate that image. For instance, on January 2, 1885, the *New York Times* called Carnegie a "Millionaire Socialist." The previous month, Carnegie had praised socialism during a speech to the Nineteenth Century Club. In attendance was John Swinton, owner and editor of *John Swinton's Paper*, a pro-labor newspaper published in New York City. Swinton published a summary of Carnegie's remarks that was later shown to the industrialist by a *New York Times* reporter. In response to the reporter's question about whether he had, in fact, praised socialism, Carnegie confirmed that he had and went so far as to say, "I believe socialism is the grandest theory ever presented, and I am sure some day it will rule the world [. . .] working people have my full sympathy, and I always lend a helping hand."[28]

The following year, Carnegie published a widely read article in *Forum* in which he asserted, "The right of the workingmen to combine and form trades-unions is no less sacred than the right of the manufacturer to enter into associations and conferences with his fellows, and it must sooner or later be conceded."[29] In 1887, he even went so far as to distribute prints of the *Forum* article to strike leaders

Initially, the contract to provide 300 tons of armor had been given to Bethlehem Steel in 1887 with a delivery date of December 1889; Bethlehem Steel failed to deliver, so Secretary of the Navy Benjamin Tracy approached Carnegie about producing 6,000 tons of steel for the Navy. Tracy assured Carnegie that, after some materials testing, there would be a sham bidding process to satisfy Congress but the company was assured of getting the contract.

who met with him to press for an eight-hour workday. The article's enthusiastic endorsement of workers' rights became, according to Carnegie Steel historian James H. Bridge, "[. . .] a veritable manual of etiquette for strikers."[30] Bridge's assertion goes a little too far; Carnegie merely claimed that strikers had the same right to form trade unions that industrialists claimed in forming monopolies and cartels designed to stifle competition. In other words, Carnegie was trying to justify his attempts to maximize profits by cornering the steel market (practices that were increasingly being criticized by the general public and members of Congress) by comparing those efforts to workers' attempts to unionize. In that sense, the article was more of a vindication of his own practices than a statement of solidarity with his workers, though, of course, Carnegie believed himself a friend of labor. However lofty his rhetoric, in practice, he showed himself to be a brutal and ruthless strikebreaker.

Carnegie was able to forgo day-to-day management of his industrial empire and indulge his literary ambitions because he had cultivated people willing to run his various companies. Though there were many, the best known (and most important for understanding the events at Homestead) was Henry Clay Frick, who at one time was called "the most hated man in America." One recent biography of Frick was subtitled "the Gospel of Greed," while the best that another (largely sympathetic) biographer called him was "the perfect capitalist."[31] While their partnership made them both unspeakably wealthy, that partnership broke down (in part due to Homestead) into a bitter feud. When Carnegie, nearing death, tried to reconnect with Frick, the latter refused and said only this: "Tell [Carnegie] I'll see him in Hell, where we are both going."

Frick is much easier to understand and interpret than Carnegie only because he was less inconsistent; Frick did not crave publicity or public approval, which freed him to ruthlessly pursue profit without subterfuge. If Frick can be said to have had a code by which he lived, it was most surely that private property was sacred and only the owner of property could choose how to dispose of it. This was a belief held by many of the men of his class and generation, but what separated Frick was his total ruthlessness in carrying that belief to its logical ends.

Henry Clay Frick was born in West Overton, a town about 40 miles southeast of Pittsburgh in Westmoreland County, Pennsylvania, on December 19, 1849. Frick's maternal grandfather was Abraham Overholt, a farmer and flour merchant who amassed a fortune through his Overholt Whiskey distillery. By contrast, Frick's father, John W. Frick, was a businessman and farmer. Though John Frick was less successful than his in-laws, his financial credit proved an essential ingredient in his son's rise to wealth and power. Frick was a sickly and weak child, and

he compensated in adolescence
and adulthood by being overly
competitive, hyper-aggressive, and
extremely ambitious. He was a
good student who, like Carnegie,

Growing up, Frick's family called him by
his middle name, "Clay."

exhibited an early and lifelong enthusiasm for reading, though unlike his
future partner, Frick had the benefit of a fair amount of formal education,
including stints at the West Overton Independent School, Westmoreland
College, and Otterbein College in Westerville, Ohio.[32]

Despite his reputation for being a "self-made man," Frick (like
Carnegie) heavily relied on assistance from others to start his empire; in
Frick's case, the assistance came in the form of family influence securing
him positions. For instance, Frick worked in his uncle's store (until he
had a falling out with his uncle's partner), and then his grandfather secured
for him a position at a cousin's distillery. Shortly thereafter, an uncle secured
for Frick a sales job at Eaton's department store in Pittsburgh.[33] The most
important instance where family money and connections helped establish
the young Frick was in the coalfields outside Pittsburgh. The growth of
industry and the explosion of the iron (and later steel) industry that was
making Andrew Carnegie wealthy in the early 1860s required fuel. At
that time, the primary fuel was coal, which was abundant in Pennsylvania.
The state's coal came in two varieties: the hard, energy-rich anthracite
found in Northeastern Pennsylvania and the softer bituminous coal found
in Western Pennsylvania. Since bituminous coal burns at a lower tempera-
ture and gives off less heat, it needed to be processed into a higher density
fuel known as coke. Using specially designed ovens, bituminous coal was
baked, driving out water, coal gas, and tar and leaving a high-carbon and
nearly smokeless fuel. The largest and best-known coking district in
Pennsylvania was Connellsville, located in Westmoreland County, a short
distance from Pittsburgh. It was here that Frick assumed his throne as the
"prince of coke."

In the late 1850s, Frick's cousin Abraham Tintsman and a partner
named Joseph Rist had purchased 600 acres of coking land outside of
Pittsburgh. In 1868, Abraham Overholt, Frick's grandfather, lent Tintsman
and Rist money to purchase a stake in Colonel A. S. Morgan's coal mines
that were located near the family distillery. Tintsman constructed coking
ovens near the mine and built tracks to ship the fuel to Pittsburgh. In
short order, the Morgan mine controlled Connellsville's coke production.
Unfortunately, the supply of coke vastly exceeded demand, and within a
year, Morgan had abandoned the operation. Worse, Tintsman was already
highly leveraged, so he would need to take on additional partners who
could supply the money necessary to continue operating the coking

operation. This is where Frick entered the picture. The future "prince of coke" arranged for his distant cousin John S. Overholt to join him in becoming Tintsman's partner. Again, family money made this possible: Frick's initial share of the capital came from a loan extended by his parents that largely came from his father's decision to mortgage the family farm. As part of the partnership, Frick agreed to serve as the mine's (unpaid) manager of the newly formed H. C. Frick & Company while simultaneously keeping his day job as the family distillery's (very well-paid) bookkeeper. In other words, Frick's rise to wealth depended largely on his family's wealth, credit, and business connections, calling into question the myth of his self-made success.

Fortune smiled on Frick. Shortly after he entered the coke business, the United States economy collapsed, and the price for a ton of coke tumbled to just under $1. Just like Carnegie, Frick cleverly exploited the depression of 1873. He acquired neighboring coal lands at a fraction of their pre-depression prices. Within a few years, as the worst of the depression receded, the price of coke climbed as high as $4 a ton (more than half of which was profit), and by the end of the decade, Frick was a millionaire. Using loans extended on the basis of his family connections, Frick continued to skillfully buy up neighboring coal lands, quickly expanding the company's coking capacity. By 1882, the company owned nine different coke works comprising more than 1,000 ovens, a sprawling empire that accounted for more than three-quarters of the coke-making facilities in Connellsville. This explosive growth made H. C. Frick & Company the largest manufacturer of coke in Western Pennsylvania and ensured the company a near monopoly when it came to providing the fuel that powered Pittsburgh's industrial growth.[34]

Frick's position as the "prince of coke" eventually brought him into contact with Carnegie and led to the formation of a partnership that would help shape the course of American industry for the remainder of the nineteenth century. Given the need for reliable high-energy fuel supplies in iron and steel production, it was no surprise that Carnegie quickly became Frick's largest and most important customer. In 1881, Frick needed capital to keep expanding, so Carnegie Brothers & Company bought an 11 percent stake in H. C. Frick & Company, making Carnegie both Frick's customer and partner. Two years later, Carnegie Brothers increased

When Frick needed additional cash, he twice solicited loans from prominent Pittsburgh banker and judge Thomas Mellon, who provided money for the company to construct additional coking ovens. Thomas Mellon was one of the founders of the Mellon Bank, which later merged with the Bank of New York.

its share to 50 percent, and by 1888, Frick was down to 21 percent (compared to Carnegie's 74 percent). Yet, Frick became enmeshed in Carnegie's steel empire as well. In 1887, Frick became a partner in Carnegie's companies. The unexpected death of Carnegie Brothers chairman David Stewart a short time later created a vacuum in the organization. Carnegie turned to Frick to fill the job, offering to loan the younger man the money to acquire a 2 percent stake in the company (and thus become eligible for election to the chairmanship). Frick agreed and was elected to the position on January 14, 1889. This proved an excellent choice: Frick increased the company's profits by an astounding 75 percent during his first year in office, but it also set in motion a series of events that culminated in the violence in Homestead less than four years later.[35]

Frick was a difficult man to work for, and he earned a reputation as a hard boss who was viscerally anti-labor. Undoubtedly, his reputation stemmed in part from the fact that he actively cheated his workers. All of his employees were required to purchase their groceries and other needs at the company stores, which routinely priced their stock 20 percent above other stores. The stores became profit generators for H. C. Frick & Company, accounting for about 8 percent of the company's profits in 1879. Employees found shopping elsewhere automatically lost their jobs. In addition, rather than pay workers in actual money, Frick simply printed his own (called "scrip," which looked similar to U.S. currency) that could only be redeemed in the company stores, further reducing the value of the workers' wages. Local businesses that depended on the workers for income were eventually forced to accept the company scrip, ensuring that they too would have to shop in Frick's company stores.[36] Frick also routinely evicted his employees from company-owned housing (that the employees rented) if they tried to unionize or went on strike. For instance, during the Great Railroad Strike of 1877, Frick enlisted the aid of the local sheriff to evict a striker from a house on land that Frick had just sold to the Baltimore and Ohio Railroad. When the striker refused to leave, Frick and the sheriff grabbed the man and threw him into the nearby creek followed shortly thereafter by the man's few possessions.[37]

Some biographers (most notably Quentin R. Skrabec, Jr.) have tried to justify Frick's actions by pointing out that such practices were not illegal, other industrialists had similar policies, and many employers treated their workers the same way. While these assertions are undoubtedly true, they miss the point: life in Frick's employ was nasty, brutal, and not infrequently short. Moreover, while practices such as these were common, it says something about Frick's ruthlessness that, in an industry characterized by shady business practices, he earned himself the reputation as the coke industry's cruelest employer.[38]

Clearly, no one was going to mistake Henry Clay Frick for a "millionaire socialist," but that served Carnegie's purposes perfectly. Frick's iron-glove approach to labor issues allowed Carnegie to present himself as the "workingman's friend" while simultaneously enjoying the increased profit margins that the "prince of coke's" hardnosed tactics made possible. For all their differences, by the mid 1880s, Carnegie and Frick were united in a single goal: ridding their companies of unions. On the surface, this made for the perfect relationship, but in hindsight, the epic collapse of their partnership in the years following Homestead is not surprising. As much as they had in common (ruthlessness, desire for profit, etc.), there was one important difference: Carnegie craved public acclaim and Frick did not. This made Carnegie act in ways that infuriated Frick, a fact that ultimately undid their partnership.

It is impossible to understand the events at Homestead without comprehending Carnegie and Frick. At the crucial junctures leading up to the events in July 1892, it was mostly their decisions that moved the situation toward its terrible climax. Yet, it is incredibly important to also understand that even Carnegie and Frick operated in a specific context that shaped their decisions by presenting them with a particular set of choices. Their shared goal of increasing profits inevitably led to confrontations with their employees that, as the next two chapters make clear, became increasingly frequent in the years leading up to Homestead.

NOTES

1   Raymond Lamont-Brown, *Carnegie: "The Richest Man in the World"* (Phoenix Mill, UK: Sutton, 2005), 1–20.
2   Peter Krass, *Carnegie* (Hoboken, NJ: John Wiley & Sons, 2002), 18–19.
3   William Serrin, *Homestead: The Glory and Tragedy of an American Steel Town* (New York, NY: Times Books, 1992), 38.
4   Lamont-Brown, *Carnegie*, 30-50.
5   Ibid., 71–83.
6   Andrew Carnegie, *Autobiography of Andrew Carnegie* (New York, NY: Houghton Mifflin, 1929), 170, quoted in Lamont-Brown, *Carnegie*, 90.
7   John K. Winkler, *Incredible Carnegie: The Life of Andrew Carnegie (1835–1919)* (Garden City, NY: Garden City Publishing, 1931), 19.
8   David Nasaw, *Andrew Carnegie* (New York, NY: The Penguin Press, 2006), 177.
9   Andrew Carnegie, "An Employer's View of the Labor Question," in *The Andrew Carnegie Reader*, Ed. Joseph Frazier Wall (Pittsburgh, PA: University of Pittsburgh Press, 1992), 97.
10 Hamlin Garland, "Homestead and Its Perilous Trades: Impressions of a Visit," *McClure's Magazine* vol. III no. 1 (June, 1894), 8.

11 Jack Beatty, *Age of Betrayal: The Triumph of Money in America* (New York, NY: Alfred A. Knopf, 2007), 348; and H. W. Brands, *The Reckless Decade: America in the 1890s* (Chicago, IL: University of Chicago Press, 2002), 130.

12 Quentin R. Skrabec, Jr., *Henry Clay Frick: The Life of the Perfect Capitalist* (Jefferson, NC: McFarland, 2010), 52.

13 Krass, *Carnegie*, 121.

14 Grosvenor quoted in John Frazier Wall, *Andrew Carnegie* (Pittsburgh, PA: University of Pittsburgh Press, 1989), 568. Lamont-Brown's statement can be found in Lamont-Brown, *Carnegie*, 157. Peter Krass' comment is in Krass, *Carnegie*, 261.

15 Harold C. Livesay, *Andrew Carnegie and the Rise of Big Business* (Glenview, IL: Scott, Foresman & Company, 1975), 131.

16 Kenneth Warren, *Triumphant Capitalism: Henry Clay Frick and the Industrial Transformation of Industrial America* (Pittsburgh, PA: University of Pittsburgh Press, 1996), 61.

17 Krass, *Carnegie*, 135.

18 Ibid., 211.

19 It should be noted that Carnegie's desire to be respected by literary men had its limits. Carnegie refused Twain's multiple requests for financial assistance over a period of years.

20 Lamont-Brown, *Carnegie*, 84.

21 Krass, *Carnegie*, 301.

22 Lamont-Brown, *Carnegie*, 51.

23 Both letters are quoted in Krass, *Carnegie*, 205.

24 James H. Bridge, *A Romance of Millions: The Inside History of the Carnegie Steel Company* (New York, NY: Aldine, 1903), vi.

25 Andrew Carnegie, *Triumphant Democracy: or Fifty Years' March of the Republic* (New York, NY: Charles Scribner's Sons, 1887), 209.

26 Carnegie to Whitney, December 8, 1866, in the Henry Payne Whitney Collection of the Papers of William Collins Whitney, Manuscript Division, Library of Congress, Washington, DC. Quoted in Nasaw, *Andrew Carnegie*, 362. Emphasis mine.

27 Nasaw, *Andrew Carnegie*, 383–384.

28 "A Millionaire Socialist," *New York Times*, January 2, 1885, 1.

29 Andrew Carnegie, "An Employer's View of the Labor Question," 96.

30 Bridge, *A Romance of Millions*, 189–193.

31 Samuel A. Schreiner, *Henry Clay Frick: The Gospel of Greed* (New York, NY: St. Martin's, 1995); and Skrabec, *Henry Clay Frick*.

32 Skrabec, *Henry Clay Frick*, 28–29.

33 Ibid., 29–34.

34 Skrabec, *Henry Clay Frick*, 35–47; and Nasaw, *Andrew Carnegie*, 210.

35 Schreiner, *Henry Clay Frick*, 54–55.

36 Ibid., 26.

37 Les Standiford, *Meet You in Hell* (New York, NY: Crown, 2005), 77.

38 Krass, *Carnegie*, 174; and Skrabec, *Henry Clay Frick*, 61.

CHAPTER 2

American Labor History, 1600–1892

A s the last chapter made clear, confrontations between Carnegie and Frick and their employees were common by the 1880s and 1890s. However, labor conflict was hardly unique to Carnegie and Frick's companies; the history of labor relations in America between the colonial era and the late nineteenth century is littered with examples of conflict. Yet, while relationships between workers and owners have been fraught for nearly four centuries, important economic changes (including the introduction of capitalism and the first and second Industrial Revolutions) increased the tension and led to more frequent confrontations. These structural changes led workers to form organizations designed to leverage their collective power in order to force wage and other types of concessions from employers. Out of these early groups emerged labor unions, which, by the Civil War, became the primary vehicle for industrial workers to assert what they considered to be their rights.

The history of American labor unionism has been shaped by at least two themes. First is that American unionism did not grow in a vacuum. Unions' success at negotiating on behalf of their members was heavily dependent upon the economic climate in which those negotiations were taking place. America's economy during the nineteenth century was characterized by a cycle of fantastic booms and catastrophic busts. When times were good, labor was in short supply, and labor unions were generally successful in achieving their goals. When the economy slid into recession (or even depression, as it did in 1819, 1837, 1857, 1873, and 1882), there were more workers than jobs, which weakened (and, in many cases, destroyed) many American unions. Nonetheless, while the story of American labor organization follows a "roller coaster" trajectory (steep climbs followed by breakneck descents), overall unions achieved some important victories during the nineteenth century that placed them at the center of labor negotiations in the United States.

A second theme is related to the first. As labor unions grew in importance in the American labor market, employers began mobilizing the state's legal and military resources to weaken these organizations. By the 1870s, the struggles between employers and employees became larger, more frequent, and more violent, a direct result of employers' growing use of state military power (i.e., militias) or private police forces such as the Pinkertons to break strikes and protect replacement workers. The last three decades of the nineteenth century saw some of the largest and most violent labor clashes in American history, including the Railroad Strike of 1877, the Haymarket Riot of 1886, and the Homestead Strike of 1892. While each of these events is important in its own right, it is important to see them not as discrete episodes, but as a chain of linked events forged by the changing economic, political, and social circumstances that both fueled the rise of labor unionism and led to violent clashes between employers and their employees.

Prior to the 1840s, workers expressed their dissatisfaction not by striking, but with periodic riots that would sweep through cities. These outbreaks of violence were usually about more than just wages or working conditions; food prices, local politics, abolitionist meetings, and other non-work issues could incite riots. Furthermore, these riots were not isolated to a specific employer or industry, and depending on the issue, employers would sometimes riot alongside their workers.[1] This is not surprising because, even as late as the early nineteenth century, most manufacturing businesses were still pretty small affairs, with the company owner working quite closely with his employees. In addition, many jobs were skilled, which meant that replacement labor was often difficult to come by; employers often could not afford to antagonize their employees.

The first recorded instance of a labor stoppage in the "New World" occurred in Jamestown in 1619. That year, a group of Polish craftsmen who had been brought to the colony at the behest of John Smith were barred by Virginia's governor from voting in the colony's election. As a result, they struck, depriving the colony of the glassware and tar (used to caulk ships). These products were incredibly important, as they were both used within the community and exported to England. As a result of the economic pressure created by the Poles' strike, Virginia's General Assembly reversed the governor's declaration. In 1636, a group of fisherman employed by an English merchant named Robert Trelawney struck after Trelawney failed to pay their wages; the outcome is not recorded. In 1677, Manhattan's carpenters struck, resulting in the first criminal prosecutions for striking in American history.

Yet, it is important to recognize that these assemblies of workers were not unions in the strictest sense. For one thing, they were only temporary, designed to deal with the specific issue of the moment. They were not designed to provide long-lasting advocacy for the workers' interests. Historian Philip Yale Nicholson has compared these early labor disputes to "[. . .] family disputes or arguments over specific issues." Conceding that these labor stoppages occasionally became violent, he concludes that they were generally treated as "personal quarrels without larger significance or connection to other disputes."[2]

An important development is that, by the 1700s, workers had begun forming clubs or fraternal societies that operated on a strictly local basis. Moreover, these were not unions per se—they were often social organizations more than anything else—but they provided some level of organization when employees sought to confront their employers. In addition, they often functioned as "mutual aid" societies, collecting funds in order to provide members with sickness and death benefits.

The Revolution facilitated organization in two ways: first, the war for independence disrupted the economic system by causing inflation, which eroded the buying power of workers' wages. Second, the revolutionaries' words—"liberty," "freedom," "justice"—encouraged the workers to demand those things from their employers. It is not surprising that, during this period, the colonies' workers also began confronting their employers. For instance, in 1768, New York's journeymen printers demanded a minimum wage. In 1786, Philadelphia's journeymen printers struck for a minimum wage, and even set up a strike fund (a pool of cash contributed by the workers to defray the costs of the strike) to support their efforts. Though they disbanded the fund after their employers met their demands, the power of coordinated action had been demonstrated. Five years later, Philadelphia's journeymen carpenters undertook the nation's first building trades strike. A few years later, the City of Brotherly Love's shoemakers formed the nation's first permanent trade union, the Federal Society of Journeymen Cordwainers. In 1799, they struck for nearly three months against wage reductions, even going so far as to pay at least one member to picket master shoemakers' shops. Though the strike was ultimately unsuccessful, it is notable for the fact that it became the first recorded sympathy strike in North American history when the city's bootmakers also refused to work in solidarity with the shoemakers.[3]

One of the most important developments for American labor was the appearance and growth of capitalism. The emergence of capitalism was closely tied to a historical event known as the "market revolution," a moment in American history when producers (farmers and artisans) shifted away from making goods largely for their own consumption to producing goods on a large scale for profit. Some historians have identified the origins of capitalism in the fourteenth century, when Europe was struck by a series of catastrophes including the Great Famine (1315–1317) and the Black Death (1348–1350) that dramatically lowered the population. Partially as a result, the continent's economic structure (called "feudalism") was weakened and gradually disintegrated, eventually giving way to mercantilism. Mercantilism, which dominated European economic thinking from the sixteenth through the eighteenth centuries, encouraged trade, the development of colonies, and domestic industries. Under mercantilism, the government aggressively pursued the nation's business interests both at home and abroad, and the dominant economic actor was the merchant, who traded commodities produced by other people. Some historians view mercantilism as an early, primitive form of capitalism while others argue that capitalism emerged only after mercantilism was called into question in the late eighteenth and early nineteenth centuries.

Capitalism, by contrast, rested on different assumptions. Basically, capitalism can be defined as an economic system where private individuals or organizations own and utilize "the means of production" (any tangible, nonhuman input used in the production process) to generate a profit. Under capitalism, industrialists displaced merchants as the primary economic actors. Both commercial and manufacturing businesses grew larger, widening the gap between employers and their employees and fundamentally altering the relationship. The apprenticeship system, under which a master in a trade took on an apprentice and, in exchange for the apprentice's labor, taught the younger man the secrets of the craft, was shunted aside as unprofitable and antiquated. Increasingly, masters used their apprentices' labor to enrich themselves and failed to pass on the secrets of their crafts, which in any case were being transformed by the introduction of machines and an ever-larger scale of production. The drive toward higher profits demanded standardization, routine, and interchangeability, the very antithesis of craft manufacture. Thus, by the early nineteenth century, "[. . .] the skilled workers soon found themselves fighting a defensive war against the mounting resources of the employers."[4]

While increased mechanization and standardization flooded the market with cheaper goods, employers were forced to compete for unskilled workers, which pushed up unskilled workers' wages. Clearly, capitalism and the market revolution eroded workers' economic and social positions by deskilling many jobs and widening the gap between employers and their employees. Workers responded by using the only tool at their disposal: collective action.

Thus, the emergence of capitalism in the early nineteenth century led to the creation of the nation's first true unions. These unions were trade unions, which meant that they united people within specific trades (i.e., carpenters or shoemakers), representing those groups' specific interests. Their memberships were small and local, reflecting the fact that the American economy was still primarily regional or local in scope. Members were usually oath-bound to follow strict rules and keep the union's proceedings secret, as well as to assist fellow society members in times of trouble. These societies sought to keep wages high and to prevent employers from hiring unskilled laborers. It was these organizations that introduced the concept of collective bargaining, which is a process whereby employers negotiate with groups of employees rather than individuals, with the goal being to strengthen employees' bargaining positions by threatening to strike if no agreement is reached.[5] Though the term "collective bargaining" was coined by Beatrice Webb, a British labor historian in 1891, it had been practiced for at least a century (recall that, as early as the 1790s, Philadelphia's shoemakers operating as the Federal Society of Journeymen Cordwainers had engaged in a form of collective bargaining). However, it was not until the early nineteenth century, when the market revolution and the emergence of capitalism had redefined employers' relationships with employees, that the use really came into its own as a tactic for workers to assert what they considered to be their rights.

The most basic form of collective action was the labor strike, which is best described as a mass refusal to work. The goal is to force employers to meet the employees' terms, since a labor stoppage costs the company owner money due to fixed costs (i.e., costs that exist for the employer regardless of how much output is produced) and lost sales. However, in order to be successful, workers engaged in a strike must prevent the employer from hiring replacement workers and resuming production. This is why striking workers often picket in front of their place of employment; the goal is to dissuade (through either persuasion or intimidation) potential replacement workers (called "scabs") from accepting employment (an action called "crossing the picket line").

Though strikes and other forms of labor stoppages in this era were largely peaceful, that was not always the case. Since collective action was a union's primary strength, any defections from its position, such as members accepting lower wages than the union was demanding, represented a threat to the entire membership's well-being. For instance, during a turnout in Philadelphia, members of the Federal Society of Journeymen Cordwainers beat up some journeymen shoemakers who had stayed on the job, reflecting the antagonism that naturally sprang up between striking workers and their replacements. This antagonism would be an enduring feature of labor stoppages throughout the nineteenth century and is partially responsible for the violence that tore apart communities such as Homestead.[6]

Naturally, the emergence and growth of labor organizations concerned employers because it limited their freedom to lower wages or increase workers' hours. Increasingly, employers turned to government for help in restraining their workers' power, a pattern that continued throughout the nineteenth century and decisively impacted later labor uprisings such as the one at Homestead. However, neither the federal nor the state constitutions said anything about the rights of workers to unionize, so employers turned increasingly to precedents from English Common Law, which had forbidden strikes since the mid eighteenth century. In 1731, an English court held that striking workers could be prosecuted for conspiracy, a precedent that placed the state's power squarely on the employers' side in labor disputes. In the nineteenth century, American courts began following suit, ruling against labor unions' rights to strike. For instance, in 1806, Philadelphia's journeymen shoemakers (who had formed the first true union less than a decade before) were dragged into court under the premise that such societies represented illegal conspiracies designed to restrain trade. *Commonwealth v. Pullis* was the first legal case in American history arising out of a labor stoppage. Eight members of the Federal Society of Journeymen Cordwainers were indicted and tried in Philadelphia's Mayor Court for conspiracy; they were convicted after a three-day trial and were fined approximately one week's wages and forced to pay the costs of the trial. Worse, from the workers' perspective, was the fact that the Federal Society of Journeymen Cordwainers was itself bankrupted by the costs of the defense, and soon ceased to exist. The precedent set by the *Pullis* decision was largely affirmed in New York three years later when a judge ruled that Manhattan's cordwainers, who had struck for higher wages, had employed methods that "were of a nature too arbitrary and coercive."[7]

Perhaps the most important aspect of the case is that, as far as the law was concerned, unions and other forms of collective bargaining were forms of "illegal conspiracies," which led to prosecutions of similar organizations in other cities during the decade that followed the *Pullis* decision. Though the court's verdict in *Pullis* was not uncontroversial (the Massachusetts Supreme Judicial Court concluded that unions were *not* illegal conspiracies in 1842), members of Pennsylvania's union were routinely indicted as conspirators in restraint of trade until the state legalized labor unions in 1869 and passed a law legalizing collective bargaining in 1872. In other words, as a result of the *Pullis* decision, America's courts became employers' primary arena for adjudicating labor disputes for the remainder of the nineteenth century.

President Andrew Jackson was called "Old Hickory" because of his physical toughness; hickory is a type of wood that has a reputation for being hard, tough, and stiff—all words that were used to describe Jackson.

Because of developments such as this, unions and their members quickly became involved in American politics at the local level, setting in motion a precedent that would define labor's approach to workingmen's rights for nearly half a century. One thing that helped the emergence of America's trade unions was the expansion of democracy associated with President Andrew Jackson's tenure in office. Called the "Jacksonian Era," this era was characterized by greater voting rights for white men, a hands-off approach to economic issues, and a desire to spread U.S. culture and government west (an outlook called "Manifest Destiny"). The symbol for this new age, Andrew Jackson, was a plantation owner and military officer who, after successfully repulsing a British attack on New Orleans in 1814, capitalized on his fame to win the presidential election of 1828. Jackson's victory was seen, then and now, as a victory for the "common (white) man" due to the fact that Jackson had come from humble origins (he was an orphan) but had risen to wealth and political power largely through his own efforts. Jackson's rise to wealth was symbolic of a number of changes taking place in American society, including westward expansion (Jackson's plantation, the Hermitage, was located in Tennessee), the expansion of voting rights to include almost all white males, and the move away from the founders' republicanism (which emphasized rule by elites) to democracy (which emphasized rule by the common man). The Jacksonians' political platform, which included opposition to corporations, central banks, and elite privilege, resonated with newly enfranchised white voters. In many ways, the values represented by the Jacksonian movement were the opposite of those that fueled capitalism, so it is not surprising that the two groups who perceived themselves as having something to lose under capitalism—namely, southern slave-owners and members of the northern working class—flocked to Jackson's party and demanded that "Old Hickory" (the president's nickname) defend their interests.

The spirit of democratic participation inaugurated by Jacksonianism encouraged workers to use their newfound political power as a tool for protecting their economic interests; this led to the formation of political organizations that promised to promote legislation designed to protect workingmen. In 1828, the first Working Men's Party was formed in Philadelphia by Thomas Skidmore. The Working Men's Party was the country's first political party formed to advocate labor reform, and it united artisans, skilled workers, and reformers. Skidmore was a machinist, teacher, and political radical who advocated redistributionist policies such as abolishing inheritance and equalizing private property. His ideas proved popular in an era when the emerging capitalist economy created both unprecedented wealth and poverty and, as a result, similar organizations sprung up in approximately 70 cities across the United States, supported by an army of papers with names such as *Working-Man's Gazette*, *Working Man's Advocate*, and *Mechanic's Free Press*. These parties advocated free public education, a 10-hour work day, and voting rights for all males while opposing imprisonment for debt and forcing state inmates to labor (because their products competed with those of non-incarcerated laborers). The Working Men's Party scored an early, and important, political victory when it managed to elect 20 of its candidates to city office in 1829, an astonishing number that represented nearly 40 percent of the contested positions that year. That same year, Working Men's Parties across New York achieved substantial electoral success, winning a series of local and municipal positions across the state. Yet, within two years, the Working Men's Parties had largely collapsed due to internal fighting and attack by both the Democratic and Federalist parties. An important legacy, however, was that while the Democrats and the Federalists succeeded in destroying the Working Men's Party, both parties were forced to adopt elements of its reform agenda, meaning that the policies (if not the party itself) lived on long after 1829.

Despite the expansion of labor unionism during this period, there were some important divisions that sapped their strength. For instance, the divide between skilled and unskilled workers weakened unions, because union organizers excluded unskilled workers from membership. In addition, America's early trade unions excluded women and African Americans (whether free or enslaved) and actively worked to keep employers from hiring these groups. Moreover, there was friction between native-born workers and immigrant laborers. Between 1830 and 1860, the number of immigrants to the United States skyrocketed. In 1830, less than 2 percent of Americans were immigrants; 20 years later, immigrants accounted for nearly 10 percent of the country's population. During the periodic economic downturns of this era, immigrants became convenient targets of workers' rage. At two points during this period (1844–1845 and 1855–1860), there appeared political parties (the Native American Party and the American Party) whose primary goal was restricting or eliminating immigration to the United States; many workers, stung by the economic downturns following the panics of 1837 and 1857, enthusiastically supported such legislation out of fear that immigrants deprived them of work. In other words, there were deep divisions in the labor movement that, as we shall see, employers such as Carnegie and Frick exploited to weaken organized labor.

The tide of labor union expansion inaugurated by the Jacksonian Era crested in 1837. Due to America's economic expansion between 1824 and 1837, labor was generally scarce, so employers were not in a position to oppose their employees' demands. When the economy sours, however, labor scarcity quickly turns into labor surplus as people are thrown out of work and are therefore willing to work for lower wages; power shifts back to employers, who are in a better position to refuse their employees' demands. The late 1830s was no exception: the economic crisis caused by the "Bank War" negatively impacted America's labor organizing. Andrew Jackson fervently opposed banks on the grounds that these institutions aided elites at the expense of the common man. He particularly hated the Second Bank of the United States, partially for political reasons, but mostly because he believed that it enriched elites at the expense of the rest of the nation's citizens. Jackson's political enemies tried to use re-chartering the Second Bank of the United States as an issue in the 1832 presidential election, during which Jackson would run for re-election. The bank was relatively popular at the moment due to the fact that the country's economy was booming. Thus, in January of 1832, Jackson's enemies introduced bills to both houses of Congress authorizing re-charter of the bank, reasoning that Jackson would have to choose between his principles and veto the bank during a period of popularity or risk being tarred as a hypocrite in the upcoming election. Jackson took their challenge, vetoing the re-charter bill in July 1832 and issuing a persuasive public message that laid out his rationale for doing so. Congress failed to overturn Jackson's veto, and it was sustained. The Bank's slow demise meant far less oversight over the nation's other banks, who relaxed their oversight standards for lending money. The increase in loaned funds fueled a period of massive economic expansion, but also created a bubble that popped in 1837, causing a massive depression that touched on almost all aspects of American life.

The economic depression that resulted from the Bank War led to higher unemployment and lower wages for workers.

In an extreme example, one-third of New York's workforce—500,000 men—lost their jobs, while industrial centers throughout the northeast saw factories and mills shuttered. Financing for roads, canals, and railroads disintegrated. In addition, the depression provoked a backlash against labor unionism; at one point, the Master Carpenters' Association of Philadelphia formed an organization called the Anti-Trades Union Association designed to break the city's trade unions. A similar organization formed in New York City to coordinate manufacturers and retailers' efforts in order to resist that city's unions. In sum, the depression weakened America's unions and eroded labor's gains well into the 1850s.[8]

The Civil War revitalized the American labor movement for a number of reasons.[9] However, in the last three decades of the nineteenth century, the average size of factories in most industries more than doubled. As factories began appearing and growing in the years leading up to the Civil War, and as manufacturers found ways to reduce production to a series of discrete tasks that did not require skilled laborers, antagonism between workers and employers grew. This narrowed the range of issues, broke down whatever solidarity may have existed between employers and employees, and shifted the scene of conflict from the neighborhood (with its broad range of political, social, and racial issues) to the smaller world of the workplace (with a narrower range of work-related issues).[10]

As a result, unions became the primary vehicle for negotiations between workers and employers; in the last decade of the nineteenth century, unions conducted 75 percent of labor strikes in the United States. As the number of union-led strikes climbed during the 1880s and 1890s, the number of sympathy strikes also increased, accounting for more than one in 10 labor stoppages in 1891.[11] Put another way, national unions that united laborers across trades made the organizations more powerful than the sum of their constituent groups and represented a greater threat to industry's ability to slash wages or increase work requirements. In addition, the war mitigated many of the divisions (particularly those regarding immigrants) that had weakened earlier unions and sapped their efficiency.

Furthermore, labor struggles became national affairs. Before the Civil War, most coalitions of workers struggled on the local level; the development of a truly national labor market in the 1870s and 1880s meant that unions needed to be national organizations if they wanted to successfully protect workers' interests. The shift toward national unions strengthened workers' positions by increasing the power of collective bargaining: larger, stronger unions could provide some wage replacement during strikes and the newer national unions became quite adept at timing labor stoppages to ensure maximum impact. The rise of unions also meant an increase in "sympathy strikes," or labor stoppages at companies not experiencing labor issues. For instance, the workers at Company A might go on strike over wages. When this happened, the workers at Company B might also call a strike, even though there was no specific issue with the management of Company B. The point of a sympathy strike was to force the management of Company B to pressure the management of Company A to settle with its workers. As such, organized labor became a serious threat to employers' power, leading to aggressive and often violent confrontations between employers and their workers.

In 1863, Ira Steward, a skilled laborer and member of the Machinists and Blacksmith's Union, formed the Eight Hour League in Boston. The organization's goal was to agitate for a legally mandated eight-hour limit to the workday, something that working men had been trying to achieve at least since the days of the Working Men's Party (that body had argued for a 10-hour day). The movement grew amazingly quickly, and within half a decade, most cities boasted a branch, which was overseen by statewide "Grand Eight-Hour Leagues." By 1867, the league had convinced four states and numerous cities to adopt eight-hour legislation, at least for women and municipal workers. The following year, the federal government adopted the eight-hour workday for all of its employees, though there were loopholes that effectively neutered the legislation.[12]

At about the same time, America's first national labor federation—the National Labor Union (NLU)—was formed. Founded in 1866, the NLU brought together a number of smaller unions, including the Coach Makers' International Union and the Machinists and Blacksmiths Union, into a larger national union that consolidated workers from a variety of industries. Contemporary estimates put the membership at anywhere between 600,000 and 800,000, though one of the leading historians of the era has called these figures greatly exaggerated.[13] According to historian Philip Yale Nicholson, the NLU was not exactly a union. Rather, it was "[. . .] a loose confederation of labor unions and reform minded organizations." As a result, there was tension from the beginning between workers, who sought to keep the NLU focused solely on bread-and-butter labor issues and those members committed to broader social reform.[14] Standing at the center of this tension was William Sylvis, president of the National Union of Iron Moulders. Sylvis was responsible for a number of important innovations (including selling union cards and improving dues collection), which improved the National Union of Iron Moulders' finances and gave the union the strength it needed to weather protracted strikes. Elected the NLU's president in 1868, Sylvis tried to expand the organization's scope from merely labor issues to a bona fide political party (similar to what the Working Men's Parties from a generation before had aspired to achieve), but his death in 1869 cut short his presidency. When leading members of the NLU formed the National Reform Party in 1872, which mixed labor issues such as the eight-hour day with more controversial reform legislation (such as advocating the creation of non-gold-backed currency, called "greenbacks"), the union split into factions, essentially killing it.

Yet, the idea of a national union that could successfully challenge the growing power of America's national corporations did not die with the NLU, and some of the union's former members hoped to reorganize another large national union to keep fighting for these issues.

In addition, there were some other important setbacks for organized labor during the years following the Civil War. Perhaps the worst was a depression between 1873 and 1879, one of the dire economic recessions that plagued America periodically during the nineteenth century. As we have seen, depressions tended to erode workers' power by creating a large surplus of labor, thereby putting employers in a position where they could offer lower wages. The Civil War had fueled massive growth in America's railroad industry, spurred by legislation such as the Pacific Railroad Acts, which authorized and funded the construction of the transcontinental railroad. Railroad growth not only created unimaginable wealth for men such as Andrew Carnegie, but also led to general prosperity. Within a few years of the war's end, America's railroads were the second largest employer behind only agriculture. Unfortunately, the massive and rapid expansion of America's rail system encouraged speculation, creating an economic "bubble" that encouraged over-investment in increasingly unprofitable rail lines.

While we do not think much about it today, during the last three decades of the nineteenth century, Americans were bitterly divided over what their money should be made of. Most Republicans advocated only coining (making into money) gold because it prevented inflation. Many Democrats and Populists, by contrast, argued that the federal government should expand the money supply by coining silver. There was even a political party—the Greenback Party—whose primary goal was to get the federal government to print paper money.

At the same time, Congress undertook a massive reorganization of the country's money system with profound results. In 1871, Germany stopped minting silver coins, which caused the demand for silver to drop. Lower demand caused silver prices to drop, hurting the nation's silver-mining industry. Congress added to the problem by passing the Coinage Act of 1873, which essentially ended U.S. government purchases of silver for use in minting dollar coins; henceforth, the United States would only coin gold. This had two effects: first, it drove down both the demand and price of silver even further; and second, it lowered the amount of money in circulation, raising interest rates and making it difficult for businesses and individuals to get credit. Investors, spooked by the rapid changes, stopped buying bonds, which only made it more difficult and expensive for America's corporations to raise capital for expansion.

Matters came to a head in September 1873, when Jay Cooke & Company was unable to sell millions of dollars in railroad bonds to move ahead with the planned construction of a second transcontinental railroad, the Northern Pacific Railway. Cooke was known as the "financier of the

Civil War" for his company's success selling government bonds during the war and for his ability to arrange loans for the Commonwealth of Pennsylvania to meet its financial obligations, all of which had made him an extremely rich man. After the war, Cooke had invested heavily in railroad development, heavily leveraging the firm's assets in order to maximize its profit. Cooke's inability to sell new railroad bonds in September 1873 damaged the firm's credit, derailing a $300 million loan from the federal government that might have kept the company afloat. As a result, on September 18, Jay Cooke & Company declared bankruptcy, which caused a cascade of bank failures throughout the United States and eventually resulted in the closure for 10 days of the New York Stock Exchange. Worse, Jay Cooke & Company had served as the conduit by which the federal government financed its portion of railroad construction, magnifying the economic effects of the company's bankruptcy. Within a year, dozens of railroad lines collapsed, which in turn caused nearly 20,000 additional business failures. Unemployment climbed over 8 percent, with some estimates putting it as high as 14 percent by 1876, and employers took advantage of the decline to cut wages and weaken organized labor.

The Panic of 1873 and the resulting depression contributed to an explosion of labor violence that had important implications for the events at Homestead. In mid 1877, the Baltimore and Ohio (B&O) railroad announced that, for the second time in a year, it was cutting wages. On July 14, workers responded by going on strike, and strikers in Martinsburg, West Virginia successfully prevented B&O from running its trains, essentially paralyzing rail traffic in the United States. Recently elected Governor Henry M. Matthews, a Democrat, called out the local militia to disperse the strike. Unfortunately for Matthews, the militiamen proved initially sympathetic to the strikers and refused to take action until being fired upon by one of the workers named William Vandergrift. The militiamen returned fire, killing Vandergrift. In the days that followed, both Vandergrift and the militia were pilloried in the local newspapers, and the militia officially notified the governor that it would no longer follow his orders. Matthews dispatched another militia company (this one carefully screened to ensure it contained no rail workers), but this company also proved sympathetic to the strikers. As a result, Matthews reached out to President Rutherford B. Hayes and requested federal assistance.

The economic slowdown caused by the Panic of 1873 is called the "Long Depression" by historians and economists. According to the National Bureau of Economic Research, the Long Depression is America's longest-lasting economic slowdown, eclipsing even the Great Depression of the 1930s!

Election of 1876

The election of 1876 pitted incumbent Republican Rutherford B. Hayes (former governor of Ohio) against the Democratic governor of New York, Samuel B. Tilden. It is one of the most controversial in American history due to the fact that the winner of the popular vote (Tilden) was not chosen by the electoral college, an outcome that has only happened four times in the nation's history. The election's outcome was ultimately decided by a deal constructed by 15 prominent Democrats and Republicans from both Congress and the United States Supreme Court. Under the "Compromise of 1877," Democrats agreed to award Hayes the presidency in exchange for the Republicans' promise that, once inaugurated, the new president would remove federal troops from former Confederate states. Once in office, Hayes kept his part of the bargain, a move that effectively ended Reconstruction because it allowed southern states to impose draconian laws that discriminated against African Americans.

Matthews' request put Hayes in a difficult position politically. During the presidential campaign of 1876, Hayes had promised not to involve the federal government in local issues, which was an attempt to reach out to Democrats and southerners unhappy about the direction of Reconstruction (or the federal government's ongoing attempt to bring the former Confederate states back into the Union). Worse, Hayes was in a precarious political position as well: he had lost the popular vote during the previous year's presidential campaign and was only placed in the White House after a "backroom" deal was worked out between Republicans and Democrats.

Less than a year into a presidency inaugurated by one of the most controversial elections in U.S. history, Hayes needed to tread lightly. Initially, he tried negotiating with the strikers but, when this proved futile, Hayes reluctantly deployed federal troops to Martinsburg. Ironically, by the time that federal troops arrived in West Virginia, the situation had calmed down; though the strike was ongoing, it was largely peaceful. By contrast, violent labor uprisings had occurred in Maryland, Pennsylvania, Missouri, and Illinois, and many Americans (who were themselves squeezed by the seemingly endless "Long Depression") expressed sympathy for the strikers. For instance, when Maryland's Governor John Carroll dispatched two regiments of the state's national guard to restore order in Baltimore, local citizens attacked the militiamen, successfully preventing the restoration of train service. The militia regiments ended up in a firefight with Baltimore citizens that resulted in the militiamen being trapped in Camden

Yards for days. In the end, President Hayes was forced to dispatch marines to the city in order to rescue the militia regiments.

While the violence spread across the United States, Pennsylvania was especially hard hit. By far, the worst site of violence was in Pittsburgh where, in an attempt to restore the Pennsylvania Railroad to profitability, company president (and Carnegie's former mentor) Thomas A. Scott had cut workers' wages, provoking a strike. In light of the violence tearing apart other railroad hubs, Scott demanded that the strikers be fed a "rifle diet" (i.e., fired upon), but, initially, local law enforcement refused (as in West Virginia) to fire on the striking railroad workers. Once the strikers began throwing rocks, however, the militia opened fire, eventually killing 20 and wounding 29. This outraged and galvanized the strikers, who forced the militiamen to take cover in a nearby roundhouse (a circular building used to turn train engines around). Infuriated by the fact that the militia had opened fire on them, the strikers went on a rampage: they set fire to dozens of buildings and destroyed more than 100 locomotive engines and over 1,000 passenger and freight cars. The next day, the militiamen decided to shoot their way of out the roundhouse, provoking another firefight that left 20 more strikers dead. Hayes was once again forced to dispatch federal troops to quell the violence, but not before the disorder had spread to industrial cities throughout the Quaker State, including Philadelphia, Scranton, and Shamokin.

The strikes raged throughout various American cities for over a month and were only quelled by the appearance of federal troops. Hayes' use of federal troops to end the strikes was a victory for the railroad companies, who maintained the wage cuts that had provoked the shutdown in the first place, though many of the railroads made token gestures to improve working conditions. More important, in the short term, the railroads did not attempt to lower wages again, likely due to the fact that the public overwhelmingly blamed them (and not the strikers) for the violence.

The generally poor outlook for workers created a great deal of discontent, which in turn led to the formation of the Knights of Labor (KOL), the largest and most important labor organization in the United States during the 1880s. Though it was established in 1869 by a handful of Philadelphia tailors, the vacuum created by the NLU's collapse in the early 1870s and the economic depression in the middle years of that decade fueled the KOL's expansion, particularly in the coalfields of Pennsylvania. By the mid 1880s, the Knights boasted nearly three-quarters of a million members. Like the NLU, the KOL advocated a series of issues; some were directly related to labor (such as the eight-hour day) while others were a little further afield (such as the organization's demand that public lands be reserved for settlers or that the federal government should expand the money supply by issuing paper money). In the words of one historian, "The Knights sought a radical transformation of the nation [. . .] through educational enlightenment and the mobilization of all producers."[15] Thus, the KOL opened membership to almost all current and former wage earners (notably, doctors, lawyers, bankers, stockbrokers, liquor sellers, and gamblers were excluded) and did not exclude women or African Americans, resulting in explosive growth. As the Knights' membership rolls swelled, the organizations lost the trappings of a fraternal organization and began functioning more like a labor union. The organization's second, and most important, "Grand Master Workman," lawyer and former Scranton mayor Terrence V. Powderly, detested strikes (at one point, he called them "barbaric," and refused to sanction work stoppages), but the KOL's decentralized structure left local lodges a great deal of autonomy.

The KOL crested at a moment when, according to one labor historian, strikes hit a "crescendo of frequency." In the first five years of the 1880s, American workers struck about 500 times annually, involving just over 100,000 workers each year. Both the number of strikes and the number of workers involved jumped substantially in 1886, when approximately 400,000 workers engaged in nearly 1,500 strikes. While this number dropped below 1,000 two years later, it was still a substantial increase from earlier in the decade. Most important, from the KOL's perspective, was the fact that a substantial number of these work stoppages were union organized and led.[16]

Yet, despite this upsurge in union activity during this period, the KOL's power (and very existence) was ebbing. The KOL, which burst onto the scene in the early 1870s, suffered a similarly spectacular decline. There were numerous reasons for the union's decline, including internal squabbles between the loosely affiliated local chapters and the fact that many employers would not hire or negotiate with KOL-affiliated workers. Moreover, while the KOL was the largest and most important labor organization in America at this time, it was not the *only* labor union, and these other organizations worked assiduously to recruit workers who, for one reason or another, did not wish to associate with the KOL. Worse, the KOL was weakened by a series of violent labor confrontations that turned violent. The most important of these was the Haymarket Riot, which gave the public the impression that the KOL was controlled by dangerous radicals, which alienated members; in the year after the Haymarket Riot, membership in the KOL in Chicago dropped from over 25,000 to 3,500.[17]

While some historians have argued that, in the long run, the Haymarket Riot aided the American labor movement, in the short run it proved disastrous for the KOL, which was widely blamed for the violence.

The Haymarket Riot

The Haymarket Riot (also called the Haymarket Massacre or the Haymarket Affair) was a seminal event in the history of American labor that, among other things, contributed to the implosion of the Knights of Labor.

The massive expansion of rail lines after the Civil War had transformed Chicago; the city's central position made it an ideal railroad terminus, which in turned spurred industrial growth that attracted hundreds of thousands of workers (native-born and immigrant) to relocate. As a result, the city's population grew by an astonishing 1,000 percent between 1850 and 1870, jumping from under 30,000 to nearly 300,000. Then, in just the 10 years between 1870 and 1880, the city added an additional 200,000 residents. Due to the presence of so many workers, Chicago became a center for union organizing, particularly over issues such as working conditions, wages, and the length of the workday.

However, the Long Depression of the 1870s exacted a heavy toll on Chicago's workingmen: as railroad construction suddenly contracted, many workers lost their jobs. Though the economy recovered slightly at the end of the 1870s, another economic slowdown that began in 1882 turned into a full-fledged panic by 1884, causing bank failures and a spike in the unemployment rate. Surplus workers gave employers an opportunity to roll back labor's gains by forcing down wages or rescinding concessions made to unions during more prosperous times. Labor responded by trying to hold onto its hard-won gains and, in October of 1884, the Federation of Organized Trades and Labor Unions (a forerunner of the American Federation of Labor, or AFL) declared that, 18 months hence, the eight-hour workday would become standard throughout industry. In anticipation of this event, local unions across the country planned strikes to force employers to accept the eight-hour day.

On May 1, 1886, somewhere between one-quarter and half a million workers struck in cities across the United States. However, it is important to emphasize that there was little coordination between these local strikes, or even between the various unions in a given city; while all were committed to the same goal (the eight-hour work day), they represented a large cross-section of industries, ethnic groups, and political persuasions. Though most of the rallies were peaceful, events outside the McCormick Harvesting Machine Company plant in Chicago set in motion a chain of events that culminated in an act of terrorism that had long-lasting repercussions for labor in the United States.

By the time of the eight-hour day rallies, McCormick's employees had been on strike for nearly three months. McCormick had replaced the striking workers with scabs who crossed the picket line each day under the protection of 400 police officers; though many of the scabs ended up joining the union, enough scabs reported for work each day that McCormick was able to continue production. Up to this point, the strike had been peaceful but, on May 3, a group of strikers confronted the scabs as the latter group left work for the day. The police fired on the strikers, killing two (though early newspaper reports placed the number as high as six). Taking advantage of the public's sense of outrage over the police officers' actions, local anarchists called for a rally at Haymarket Square, a busy commercial area. Initially, the anarchists' fliers, which were printed in English and German, beseeched workers to "arm themselves" and "appear in full force," though this language was later toned down to appease more conservative union members.

The following evening, a crowd of between 600 and 3,000 people appeared in the Haymarket Square. A series of speakers lectured the crowd and, while some of the speeches appealed for radical action, the meeting was non-violent. Around 10:30 p.m., however, things took a turn for the worse when a small army of Chicago policemen arrived to break up the event. Someone threw a homemade bomb into the police officers' path and the resulting explosion killed seven officers and a handful of civilians. Confusion begat more violence, as gunfire broke out between the police and the crowd (no one is sure who fired the first shot), resulting in at least 60 officers and an unknown number of civilians (many of whom feared being arrested if they sought medical attention) being injured. In the days that followed, the police raided the offices of *Arbeiter-Zeitung* (*"Workers' Times"*) and arrested the newspaper's editor, August Spies, a labor activist who had spoken at Haymarket shortly before the bomb exploded. He and seven other defendants were tried for murder. All were convicted, with seven being sentenced to death and one (Oscar Neebe) being sentenced to 15 years. On November 11, 1887, after commutations and a suicide, four of the defendants—August Spies, George Engel, Adolph Fischer, and Albert Parsons—were executed.

Though the KOL repudiated violence as a means for achieving its goals, negative press coverage implied that the union encouraged violence and radicalism. This perception was reinforced when KOL strikers resorted to violence in a strike against Union Pacific and Missouri Pacific railroads in the spring and summer of 1886. Worse, members of the Brotherhood of Engineers refused to strike and continued working, weakening the KOL. The following year, striking KOL workers in Thibadoux, Louisiana were massacred by vigilantes; while this was largely about race (the strikers were mostly black while the vigilantes were all white), it nonetheless demoralized the union and reinforced the sense that the KOL was on the decline. By 1890, membership in the organization had declined by approximately 90 percent and employers had become emboldened by the sense that they could simply break strikes by appealing to state governors for militia units.

The KOL's death, much like the NLU's almost 15 years before, created a vacuum that would be filled by a new labor organization, in this case the American Federation of Labor (AFL). Founded in 1886, the AFL was designed to provide industrial workers an alternative to the KOL, representing those unions not affiliated with the Knights. According to historian Leon Wolff, America's capitalists were far more worried about the AFL than the KOL because the former union was large, its leadership was willing to strike, and it was "[. . .] not led by a collection of nebulous gasbags."[18] In contrast to the KOL, the AFL's goals were narrower and much more conservative: under its first president, Samuel Gompers, the AFL focused solely on "bread and butter" issues such as wages, hours, and working conditions. With the exception of a brief time in the 1890s, Gompers led the union from 1886 to his death in 1924. Though he had flirted with socialism as a young man, Gompers had become more conservative, and the union's goals reflected it. Whereas socialists sought the community ownership of property, the AFL advocated that workers make peace with capitalism and demanded only that they receive wages sufficient to enjoy an "American" standard of living.

This narrower vision of "labor issues" was a repudiation of more than 50 years of union engagement with the political sphere, a tradition that dated back to the Jacksonian Era.

In addition, unlike the KOL, the AFL discriminated against African Americans, women, and radicals, all of whom were barred from membership in the new organization. Consequently, the AFL grew more slowly than the KOL, only reaching 250,000 members in the early 1890s. The union also reflected the nativist prejudices of the day and refused to admit immigrants; this was a particularly absurd policy given that a substantial percentage of the millions of immigrants who came to the United States in the latter half of the nineteenth century worked in the country's factories, mines, and workshops, making them ideal potential union members. By excluding them, the AFL made it possible for employers to exploit ethnic differences (i.e., by refusing to negotiate with striking workers and instead replacing the strikers with immigrants) and thereby weaken the labor movement. This is a strategy that both Frick and Carnegie employed to maximum effectiveness in the years leading up to Homestead. Nevertheless, the AFL quickly became a powerhouse, representing thousands of American workers.

One of the most important and potent of the AFL's affiliated unions was a craft union known as the Amalgamated Association of Iron and Steel Workers; the AAISW, as it was known, accounted for almost one-tenth of the AFL's membership in 1892.[19] The conservative AAISW's philosophy —focusing on wages and working conditions in order to secure for its members an "American" lifestyle—was fully in line with the AFL's goals. As its name suggests, the AAISW represented steel and ironworkers, including those working at a large Carnegie Steel plant in a small mill town outside of Pittsburgh called Homestead.

NOTES

1   David Montgomery, "Strikes in Nineteenth-Century America," *Social Science History* vol. 4 no. 1 (Winter, 1980), 81–104.

2   Philip Yale Nicholson, *Labor's Story in the United States* (Philadelphia, PA: Temple University Press, 2004), 20.

3   Philip S. Foner, *History of the Labor Movement in the United States, Vol. I* (New York, NY: International Publishers Co., Inc., 1988), 71.

4   Foster Rhea Dulles and Melvyn Dubofsky, *Labor in America* (Arlington Heights, IL: Harlan Davidson, Inc., 1984), 26.

5   Ibid., 27.

6   Ibid., 29.

7   Stanley L. Engerman, ed., *Terms of Slavery: Slavery, Serfdom, and Free Labor* (Stanford, CA: Stanford University Press, 1999), 223; and Nicholson, *Labor's Story in the United States*, 48.

8   Nicholson, *Labor's Story in the United States*, 74–75.

9   Joshua L. Rosenbloom, "Strikebreaking and the Labor Market in the United States, 1881–1894," *The Journal of Economic History* vol. 58, no. 1 (March, 1998), 188.

10   Montgomery, "Strikes in Nineteenth-Century America," 88.

11   Ibid., 88–92.

12   Nicholson, *Labor's Story in the United States*, 98.

13   Philip S. Foner, *History of the Labor Movement in the United States, Vol. I* (New York, NY: International Publishers Co., Inc., 1988), 377.

14   Nicholson, *Labor's Story in the United States*, 100.

15   Ibid., 116.

16   Ibid.

17   Philip S. Foner, *History of the Labor Movement in the United States, Vol. II* (New York, NY: International Publishers Co., Inc., 1988), 160.

18   Leon Wolff, *Lockout: The Story of the Homestead Strike of 1892* (New York, NY: Harper & Row, Publishers, 1965), 16.

19   Ibid., 17.

CHAPTER 3

Lead-up to the Strike

People tend to think of the events at Homestead as a single, discrete episode in the history of American labor relations. In reality, as the last chapter demonstrated, the violence that rocked Homestead in July 1892 was the culmination of a series of changes reshaping American industry and society at the end of the nineteenth century. On the one hand (as shown in Chapter 1), individual personalities were crucial to the way events at Homestead unfolded; remove either Carnegie or Frick from the mix, and things might have turned out very differently. On the other hand, individual actors make choices in a very specific context that limits their options and makes certain outcomes likelier than others. It is crucial, therefore, to understand the context that gave rise to the events at Homestead and to see what happened there not as a single event, but rather an episode in a larger struggle between labor and industry that (as the last chapter described) had been taking place for years.

The last 30 years of the nineteenth century was a period of great transition and uncertainty for business and labor alike. The United States was rocked by three recessions during this period (1873–1877, 1883–1885, and 1893–1897), resulting in extensive business failures and prolonged periods of unemployment.[1] Until the 1930s, historians called this period "the Great Depression" because the years of economic contraction actually exceeded those of expansion. This was America's "Gilded Age," a period of population growth and accumulation of wealth on a scale larger than at any time in American history up to that point. While the well connected could get outrageously wealthy, often their success came at the expense of millions of other people who lived on the very edge of abject poverty. This state of affairs contributed to increasingly antagonistic relationships between employees and employers.

The increased power of national unions representing multiple trades over regional and trade unions helps explain Carnegie's increasingly aggressive anti-unionism in the 1880s and 1890s. Unlike Frick, who uniformly opposed unions throughout his career, Carnegie's position was much more fluid. In 1886, he asserted, "My experience has been that trades-unions, upon the whole, are beneficial to both labor and capital. They certainly educate the working-men, and give them a truer conception of the relations of capital and labor than they could otherwise form."[2] As Chapter 1 revealed, part of this was due to Carnegie's disingenuous nature: he frequently said one thing and did another throughout his career. However, his position on unions was more complicated than this. He strongly supported unions *when they helped him make money*, as they did up until the mid 1880s. Until then, Carnegie's perspective was that unions provided him an advantage over his competitors by providing a dependable workforce of skilled workers. Furthermore, when he negotiated a wage rate with his workers, that rate quickly became the standard wage paid throughout most of the industry, driving up his competitors' costs. Since Carnegie had a significant technological advantage over his competitors and Pittsburgh was close to all the necessary raw material, he could still afford to pay the higher wages *and* undersell them. Meanwhile, the wages he was paying became an industry standard, discouraging potential competitors without his technological and geographic advantages. As historian David Brody has noted, the Amalgamated Association of Iron and Steel Workers (AAISW) served as a "stabilizing" force in the "chaotic" steel and iron industry, and that stability was useful to Carnegie, who had numerous competitive advantages over other mills.[3] In this sense, strong unions and reasonable wages made good business sense for Carnegie, at least until the mid 1880s.[4]

Two factors changed his opinion: (1) technological innovations that made skilled workers less necessary; and (2) the emergence of a national labor market that made it more expensive to produce steel. New technology meant that producing steel, a process that had been composed of multiple steps requiring highly skilled workers at each juncture, could now be performed by people with fewer skills and less training. According to historian Jonathan Rees, iron puddling was a highly skilled craft that took between one and two years to learn, but unskilled laborers could learn steelmaking in as little as six weeks.[5] Thus, by the mid 1880s, it became feasible to simply replace striking workers because unskilled laborers were plentiful, and they could quickly and easily be trained. As the next section outlines, this became Carnegie and Frick's preferred tactic for dealing with labor stoppages in the late 1880s and 1890s.

Amalgamated Association of Iron and Steel Workers (AAISW)

The Amalgamated Association of Iron and Steelworkers (AAISW) was a labor union formed in Pittsburgh on August 4, 1876. The AAISW was formed out of a number of regional labor unions representing workers in various parts of the iron and steel industry, including the United Sons of Vulcan, the Associated Brotherhood of Iron and Steel Heaters, the Rollers and Roughers of the United States, and the Iron and Steel Union Roll Hands' Union. Initially, the AAISW only had about 3,000 members, but in the 16 years between its founding and the violence at Homestead, membership swelled to about 24,000, with lodges in Pittsburgh, Chicago, Youngstown, and other industrial centers. Within a decade, the AAISW was the steel industry's most powerful labor union, and in 1887 the organization was united with four other labor unions in the American Federation of Labor.

Initially, the AAISW only allowed skilled workers to join; the unskilled or semiskilled were barred from membership for more than a decade, which slowed the organization's growth. Until the organization amended its constitution in 1889, the AAISW represented only the skilled laborers who made up a minority of the iron and steel industry. Dropping the prohibition on unskilled labor proved a boon to the AAISW, whose membership reached a peak of 24,068 in 1891, but tensions between skilled and unskilled workers persisted during this period.

One of the most important facts about the AAISW was that it was an avowedly "conservative" and nonviolent union, meaning that its leadership preferred negotiation and compromise. In practice, this meant that the union tried to work with ownership, rather than confront it, to protect workers' rights with the least friction possible. The defeat at Homestead was a major setback for the AAISW: membership dropped drastically, and Carnegie and Frick were successfully able to defeat membership drives at their mills throughout the 1890s. Worse, from the union's perspective, was that Carnegie and Frick's actions gave other iron and steel mill owners "cover" for their own union-busting activities, and by the end of the century not a single steel mill in Pennsylvania was unionized. For the next 30 years, the union was largely impotent, until the National Industrial Recovery Act (1933) fueled a surge in union organizing that restored some of the AAISW's former power.

By the early 1880s, the nature of iron and steel strikes was changing as well, which would have important consequences for what happened at Homestead. Construction of new lines of railroad track, which had grown considerably in 1881 and 1882, slowed in 1883 and 1884 before falling to the lowest point of the decade in 1885, causing a minor economic slowdown that shuttered 22 national banks. In 1882, nearly 90 percent of the nation's output of steel went into rails, but less than a decade later that number had shrunk to less than 50 percent.[6] The collapse in the rail market led to the consolidation of three formerly independent competitors into the Illinois Steel Company in 1889 and meant that Carnegie no longer had the world's largest production capacity. Carnegie responded by spending millions to upgrade his facilities to recapture his title, but that move only made the fundamental problem—overproduction—worse.[7] As a result, both the price *and* the profit margin on rails dropped, and Carnegie was forced to find other ways to assure that the company remained profitable. One of the most basic ways to achieve that goal was to cut costs, and one of the highest costs was labor.

Carnegie's guiding principle throughout his career was to worry about costs, and the profits would take care of themselves. As a consequence, he relentlessly sought ways to shave pennies off his production costs so that he could undersell his competition. Consequently, wages were treated as just another cost to be relentlessly driven downward, which led to callousness among management about the consequences of their decisions. Between 1878 and 1898, Carnegie cut the price of producing steel rails at Edgar Thomson Steel by 66 percent largely by forcing down the cost of labor (either through outright wage cuts or the purchase of machinery that eliminated jobs). Historian David Brody compared the hourly wages of workers at the Cambria Steel Company and found that most unskilled jobs paid less per hour in 1890 than in 1880. Moreover, Brody explored the tonnage rates paid to skilled workers at the same plant and found that these were uniformly lower in 1890 than 10 years before, some by as much as 84 percent! While Cambria was not a Carnegie steel plant, the same trend was visible across the industry. During the same period, Carnegie was able to cut the cost for producing a ton of steel by 50 percent in large part due to aggressively cutting wages.[8] Carnegie and Frick, who made their fortunes largely through economies of scale and ruthless cost-cutting, became the models for this approach to business.

Not surprisingly, the relentless drive to push wages ever lower led to a backlash among workers, which led to strikes, lockouts, and violence. The history of this period is punctuated by a number of incredibly violent labor uprisings, including the Great Railroad Strike (1877), the Haymarket Riot (1886), and, of course, Homestead (1892). One historian called it "an era of unprecedented turbulence in the history of labor relations."[9] Peter Krass notes that there were more than 22,000 strikes during the five years between 1881 and 1886, and a brief glance at the history of Carnegie's companies and H. C. Frick & Company demonstrates that the late 1880s was a particularly turbulent time for labor relations.[10] Specifically, one or

One-quarter of all strikes between 1881 and 1905 occurred in the Keystone State, due in part to the fact that the state legislature passed legislation in 1891 establishing employees' right to strike for better wages and protecting unions from indictments for conspiracy.

both companies had some form of labor trouble nearly every year between 1885 and 1892, the year of the Homestead Strike. It is therefore essential to understand the events at Homestead not as a unique event, but rather as part of a series of ongoing labor troubles caused by Carnegie and Frick's attempts to boost profits by cutting wages and exacting higher output from their employees.

In his autobiography, published posthumously in 1920, Carnegie called Homestead "the one really serious quarrel with our workmen in our whole history."[11] That was another example of Carnegie being disingenuous; in fact, he had periodically faced strikes throughout his career. According to an early history of Carnegie Steel, the company's first strike occurred in 1867. Carnegie had tried to reduce his puddlers' wages, and they responded by striking. A sudden boom in iron made it profitable for Carnegie to rehire his men at the old wages, but he took this course only *after* trying to import cheaper foreign labor. Since Carnegie was obsessed with his public image and committed to ensuring a healthy profit margin, he preferred negotiating with his workers where possible and relying on passive tactics (such as lockouts and mill shutdowns), but he was not above employing the more aggressive tactics that Frick favored.

For instance, the economic slowdown following the Panic of 1873 prompted the Association of Iron Manufacturers (a cartel that included Carnegie and other mill owners) to try to reduce their workers' wages in late 1874; when the men refused to accept the reductions, Carnegie and the other mill owners shut down their works and locked the workers out, throwing 40,000 men out of work in the middle of an economic depression. This actually worked to the advantage of Carnegie and the other mill owners because the lockout allowed them to reduce their payrolls and sell off excess stock during the downturn. However, to keep the pressure on the workers, Carnegie and the other mill owners successfully pressured local authorities to keep the workers off public relief (cash or food support given to the unemployed, the sick, and children). The owners also convinced companies to fire the locked-out workers they had hired, ensuring that these workers would have no outside sources of income. Eventually, rising economic demand exhausted Carnegie's stock of steel and forced him to rehire many of his former workers, undercutting his colleagues in the Association of Iron Manufacturers.[12] Thus, in addition to showing his colors as a strikebreaker, Carnegie demonstrated to his cartel colleagues that he simply could not be trusted.

The pace of labor disruptions picked up in the mid 1880s, with either Frick or Carnegie experiencing some troubles with their employees nearly every year. In December 1884, around the time that the company's contract with the AAISW was set to expire, the superintendent of the Edgar Thomson works, Captain William R. "Bill" Jones, posted a sign notifying the employees that the works would be shut down indefinitely so that the company could install new machinery. Some historians have seen Jones (a Welshman who had achieved the rank of captain in the Civil War and continued using the title after the war) as a "pro-labor" counterweight to Carnegie and Frick; in this interpretation, Jones' death in 1889 was partially responsible for the increasingly aggressive tactics the company employed in the late 1880s and 1890s. This, however, is a gross misinterpretation. While Jones commanded his men's respect, and although he may have liked them as individuals, his main concern was producing the greatest quantity of steel at the lowest possible cost. Thus, Jones did not reopen the mills for more than six weeks, and when he did, he made it clear that he would rehire workers only after they signed an ironclad agreement not to join any union while in Carnegie's employ. Naturally, many of the men quit the union, hoping to secure work when the mill resumed production, effectively breaking the union's presence at Edgar Thomson. Worse, the newly installed machinery and the move to 12-hour shifts cut Edgar Thomson's skilled workforce by 20 percent, ensuring a competition for jobs that militated against any future union activity.[13] Adding insult to injury, during what amounted to a Christmastime lockout, Carnegie delivered his infamous speech to the Nineteenth Century Club extolling the virtues of socialism; these comments were widely printed in newspapers in early January 1885, leaving the public with an image of Carnegie far removed from reality.

The following year, labor troubles rocked H. C. Frick & Company. In early 1886, a substantial number of Frick's workers struck over accusations that the company was underreporting coke tonnage (i.e., cheating the men) and because the company store was taking advantage of the workers and their families. The strike quickly spread to other coke producers, who often treated their workers the same way, and 75 percent of the region's coke ovens shut down. Frick responded by moving to evict his workers from company-owned housing, which only increased tensions. Riots ultimately broke out, and at the Morewood mine, Frick's men fired at the striking workers, killing one and injuring a few others. Eventually, the men returned to work in exchange for a return to 1884 wage levels, but the peace was short-lived.[14] About a year later, the Coke Syndicate proposed an industry-wide wage scale that potentially lowered workers' pay, which the workers refused to accept. Moreover, Frick's workers responded by demanding a wage *increase*. A national arbitrator was brought in, who recommended a 10 percent wage increase, about half of what the workers demanded. The workers responded by refusing and going on strike. The Coke Syndicate was emboldened by the Knights of Labor's declaring the strike illegal based on the workers' refusal to abide by the arbitrator's ruling. As a result, the national body refused to support the strikers. As Peter Krass puts it, "the usual shenanigans followed: rallies, more negotiations, imported strikebreakers, scab-related violence, and the hiring of Pinkertons."[15] Clearly, labor relations at H. C. Frick & Company had fallen into a pattern as early as the late 1880s, an eerie preview of the strategy Frick would set in motion at Homestead.

Despite substantial pressure from the other members of the Coke Syndicate (who feared labor troubles of their own if H. C. Frick & Company capitulated), Frick (reluctantly) gave in to the workers' demands on orders from Carnegie, who now owned a majority of the company's stock.

The strike endangered Carnegie's supply of fuel, and he would soon be forced to shut down his furnaces (which could irreparably damage the equipment). Undoubtedly, Carnegie was also concerned about his reputation as a benevolent employer. Frick was furious at being ordered to settle the strike but was constrained by his zealous attachment to the concept of private property; Carnegie owned the majority of the company's stock, so he called the shots. Frick responded by resigning as president of H. C. Frick & Company. However, after a private meeting with Carnegie, Frick was reinstated as president of the company a few months later. Nonetheless, the episode soured relations between the two, and Frick never fully trusted Carnegie again.[16] This is likely one of the reasons why Frick accepted the chairmanship of Carnegie, Phipps & Company when it was offered to him the following year: he could keep a close eye on Carnegie and prevent the "silver-haired devil" from sacrificing H. C. Frick & Company's interests in the name of increasing Carnegie's various steel companies' profits.

In retrospect, these events set the groundwork for what happened at Homestead. Carnegie's decision to settle the coke strike on the workers' terms meant that Carnegie Brothers & Company (one of Carnegie's other steel companies) was paying considerably more for coke than its competitors, increasing its cost of business and threatening its market advantages. As noted previously, Carnegie was pro-labor when unions helped him make a profit. After 1887, the unions in Frick's coke fields were costing Carnegie Brothers & Company money, leading Carnegie to

Pinkertons

The term "Pinkertons" refers to employees of the Pinkerton National Detective Agency, a company that provided private security and detective services. Founded in 1850 by Scottish immigrant Allan Pinkerton (1819–1884), the agency rose to national prominence during the Civil War when Pinkerton briefly served as head of the Union Intelligence Service, during which time he allegedly foiled an assassination plot against Abraham Lincoln. This rocketed the company to national fame, and soon Allan Pinkerton's name became a household word.

As a result of these and other successes, the Pinkerton National Detective Agency became synonymous with private detectives in the United States. The company's logo, a giant eye above the legend "We Never Sleep," even gave birth to the slang term for a private detective, "private eye." As private security forces in post-Civil War America, the Pinkertons filled a vacuum caused by America's antiquated law enforcement institutions. Urban police departments were a relatively new thing (the first modern police force was founded in Boston in 1838) and many towns and villages continued relying on sheriffs, an office that was clearly inadequate to deal with the large-scale labor uprisings that began taking place in the 1870s, 1880s, and 1890s. In 1865, Pennsylvania's coal and iron companies successfully lobbied the General Assembly to create the Coal and Iron Police, an organization officially designed to protect company property, but which also served to break strikes; the Coal and Iron Police were initially placed under the supervision of the Pinkerton Detective Agency, which is one of the reasons why Pinkerton agents played such a large role in the labor uprisings of this period. Indeed, the Pinkertons were first used as strikebreakers in 1866, which did not go well. As a result, Allan Pinkerton stopped accepting labor contracts for a time, but strikebreaking and union busting proved so profitable that, by the 1880s, his sons began soliciting these lucrative contracts. By the time of the Homestead Strike, Pinkertons were routinely used for strikebreaking activities by a variety of corporations. The Pinkerton agency employed undercover "spies" in various unions, and these agents were not above fomenting violence in order to give coal or iron and steel owners an excuse for violently suppressing unions. Pinkerton charged individuals and companies $5 per day per detective; the detectives themselves earned about $1 a day, a pretty low wage even by the standards of the time.

second-guess himself about pressuring Frick to end the strike.[17] Moving forward, Carnegie would allow Frick (who had recently become a shareholding partner in Carnegie's steel empire) to deal with labor troubles in his own way while maintaining enough distance to plausibly claim that he (Carnegie) did not know what the "prince of coke" had been doing.

Carnegie had his own labor problems in February 1888. He had seen an opportunity to break the AAISW at Edgar Thomson Steel, and he was determined to take it. He and Jones hoped that the shutdown would allow them to break the union by rehiring a smaller workforce of non-union laborers. In addition to imposing the sliding scale (under which workers were paid according to the price of iron or steel and which the workers accepted), Carnegie decided to move from three shifts to two, so the "lucky" workers now had 12-hour shifts rather than eight (an increase of 50 percent), which allowed him to cut his workforce substantially. In addition, Carnegie announced that employees would have to sign the contract as individuals, essentially doing away with collective bargaining, which was the basis of the union's ability to negotiate. When the workers refused to accept these terms, Carnegie ordered a lockout and began scouting for scab labor.

In March of that year, some of the striking workers went by train to New York to reason with Carnegie. There, he offered the men a tour of New York and fed them a lavish meal. He would, however, make no agreements, saying only that he planned to go to Braddock and speak to the men directly. He did give the workmen copies of his 1886 *Forum* article "An Employer's View of the Labor Question," which endorsed employees' rights to unionize and suggested that wages be tied to the prices employers charged for finished goods, seemingly making his employees "partners" in the company.[18] Yet, Carnegie's next move belied any sort of partnership. In mid April, with the lockout still in effect, Jones announced that the works would reopen on Monday, April 23. Unbeknownst to the workers, Carnegie ordered Jones to hire Pinkertons to guard the works; this private army arrived on April 22, the day before the works were to reopen. Under pressure from the company, Allegheny County Sheriff Alexander McCandless deputized 50 men and deployed them to Braddock as a barrier between the Pinkertons and workers. This allowed Carnegie to safely import workers into Braddock, a move that broke the workers' resolve. By the beginning of May, enough men had accepted the company's terms that Jones was able to restart production.

This series of events was the perfect illustration of Carnegie's approach to dealing with labor, which by the late 1880s had more or less settled into a pattern. First came the demands that, in addition to representing major wage concessions, essentially ended collective bargaining. When his employees resisted or simply refused to accept his terms, Carnegie's next move was to lock them out, which, in an era of declining prices for steel rails, could actually be economically helpful to the company. If the lockout dragged on long enough (and looked to hurt the company's profits), Carnegie (despite what he later claimed) simply imported new workers, encouraging them to violate what he called labor's central commandment: "Thou shalt not take thy neighbor's job." If the workers reacted, or looked likely to react, to the lockout or importation of new workers with violence, Carnegie enlisted law enforcement (in this case, Pinkertons) to protect the works and his new workers. This, in summary, describes Carnegie and Frick's strategy for de-unionizing the Homestead works in 1892. However, as the next two chapters exhibit, things did not work out quite as they had planned.

Part of the reason why this strategy caused so many problems in 1892 had to do with events three years earlier at Homestead. The plant had a long history of labor unrest (explored in the next chapter), so it is not surprising that the workers and management were often at cross-purposes. In the summer of 1889, Carnegie had trouble with the workmen at Homestead. The six AAISW lodges at Homestead, representing about a quarter of the site's workforce, were the strongest and most powerful arm of organized labor in the entire Carnegie empire, and they used that clout to negotiate a very favorable contract: skilled workers were paid on a tonnage rate, meaning that as the tons of steel produced went up, so did the workers' pay. About six weeks before the June 30 expiration of the contract, William Abbott, chairman of Carnegie, Phipps & Company, proposed to bring wages in line with those paid at Edgar Thomson through an immediate reduction of pay by 25 percent, a sliding scale for future wages, and the implementation of individual contracts.[19] The AAISW vigorously opposed any attempt to impose a sliding scale pay structure on the Homestead works, which would have entailed a pay cut for the works' skilled workers. Moreover, individual contracts essentially meant the end of the union since workers would no longer be able to collectively bargain. The AAISW responded by striking, and on July 1, the works fell silent.

Convinced that he could simply wait the workers out, Carnegie had ordered Abbott to keep the works closed rather than fight with the union. The company in general, and Carnegie in particular, had taken quite a beating in the press over the lockout at Edgar Thomson the previous year, so Carnegie (ever sensitive to how he was perceived by the public) wanted to shape the narrative so that there could be no doubt that it was his workers, and not he, who was responsible for any work stoppage. Abbott disobeyed Carnegie's order. Instead of waiting the workers out, he advertised for scab labor and, at the same time, secured 100 Pinkertons in case the workers tried to prevent the scabs from entering the works.

When Sheriff McCandless and more than 100 of his deputies escorted a small group of scab workers to the works on July 10, they confronted a group of nearly 2,000 striking workers who booed and threw rocks as the scabs tried to leave the train. The sheriff decided not to challenge the strikers and the train left, averting what might have been an extremely bloody showdown. Two days later, however, McCandless tried to re-enter the town, this time with a force of 125 deputies. He was again prevented from leaving the train, this time by an even larger force of striking workers and townspeople. By this point, he knew that trying to enter the town a third time would be futile and would most likely result in violence, a fact he most likely communicated to Abbott. What made things worse for Abbott were the workers at the Edgar Thomson works grumbling that they too would strike in sympathy with the workers at Homestead, no doubt in the hope of improving their own contracts.

In a panic, Abbott agreed to negotiate with the AAISW, and the parties reached a fateful compromise: the AAISW accepted the sliding scale in exchange for Carnegie, Phipps & Company accepting the concept of collective bargaining and recognizing the AAISW as the skilled Homestead workers' sole representative. The company and the union signed a three-year contract set to expire on July 1, 1892. The contract cemented the AAISW's position at Homestead so strongly that it dictated who was hired and fired at the works.[20] While the workers and the AAISW were quite pleased with the compromise, Carnegie was not. In a letter to Abbott, he complained that the compromise was made under duress and it legitimized the practice of negotiating with "lawbreakers."[21] In a sense, the company had won the skirmish (it got the workers to accept the sliding scale) but lost the battle over collective bargaining. For the next three years, Homestead would continue to operate as a union shop, a bad example (from Carnegie's perspective) for the company's other works. Carnegie and Frick were unhappy with the resolution and, even before the ink was dry, planned on aggressively rolling back these concessions in 1892. The workers, by contrast, were just as committed to protecting and, if possible, expanding their gains. In such a situation, conflict was all but inevitable.[22] Seen in this light, it should be no surprise that violence erupted when the contract expired in 1892.

At the end of 1890, trouble loomed at Edgar Thomson. The price for rails had declined precipitously and the men's pay followed until they were earning starvation wages because the sliding pay scale at Edgar Thomson had no minimum. These developments served as a warning to other plants that were on the sliding scale, galvanizing Carnegie's workers to demand a floor below which wages would not fall. The contract signed with each of the men in mid 1888 expired on December 31, and some of the men threatened to strike unless the works returned to eight-hour shifts and wages were increased. In a report to Frick, works superintendent Charles Schwab argued that the men's demands should be seriously examined given that furnace output at Edgar Thomson had increased between 25 and 30 percent, but Frick dismissed it; he had no intention to raise wages or return to the eight-hour shift. While doing so would have cost the company slightly more than $28,000 per year (0.006 percent of the $4.8 million in profits the company generated in 1890), there was a principle at stake that far exceeded the actual cost of concessions, and Frick feared that any compromise would set an awful precedent for future negotiations.[23]

Frick refused to negotiate with the men (a hallmark of his approach to labor relations), so on New Year's Eve, workers began walking off the job. That same day, a group of 60 strikers appeared in the company's stockyards, vandalizing the building and beating employees who decided not to join them. After three hours, Schwab drove the strikers away with the help of club-wielding non-strikers. On New Year's Day, a group of about 250 striking workers returned to the works and drove out (through a mix of persuasion and intimidation) the men still working. Frick responded by contacting the sheriff, who traveled to Braddock by the next available train. Supported by more than 100 Carnegie men (some armed with Winchester repeating rifles and quickly deputized), the sheriff and his crew quickly intimidated the men into returning to work. By the end of January 1891, "[. . .] the protests at Edgar Thomson were a distant memory."[24]

The following month, labor troubles rocked the entire Connellsville region and largely shut down H. C. Frick & Company's coke works. This was the infamous Morewood Massacre, an uprising that was bloodier than even Homestead. Ten thousand workers struck in February over wages and hours. The United Mine Workers of America (UMWA), a labor union that had formed the previous year and represented many of the strikers, demanded an eight-hour workday and pay increases. The miners had chosen a particularly poor time to push for pay increases: the prices for steel and rails had dropped in the months leading up to the strike, so cutting production worked to the company's advantage. Moreover, Frick had anticipated the trouble and had set aside a few months' worth of extra coke in order to wait out the strikers. In other words, the strike actually benefited Carnegie Brothers & Company and, by extension, H. C. Frick & Company, strengthening Frick's resolve to wait the strikers out, at least in the short run.[25]

As the strike dragged on, however, Frick got more aggressive. On March 26, he posted his terms: a nine-hour workday and a sliding scale that, in an era of depressed

The United Mine Workers was formed in Columbus, Ohio in January 1890. It was not the first miners' union, but it was one of the most successful, eventually winning the eight-hour workday in 1898.

In January 1891, a mine cave-in killed 109 miners, a poignant reminder of how dangerous their jobs were.

coke prices, was a particularly bitter pill for the workers.

This tactic did not work as well as Frick had hoped. By the end of the month, the company was operating at about 30 percent of its normal production levels. Frick decided to go further, evicting workers from company-owned housing, which only increased their anger toward the company and sense of solidarity with one another. Even one of Frick's most sympathetic biographers, Quentin R. Skrabec Jr., characterized this move as counterproductive and "hardheaded."[26] Carnegie had advised against confronting the workers until April because he believed that the men would be forced by desperation to return to work, thus preventing the need for any violence; he feared that forcing the issue would lead to violence, and he was right. It is important to note, however, that while Carnegie and Frick differed on tactics, both remained committed to resisting the union's demands.

In response to Frick's refusal to negotiate, approximately 1,000 strikers formed themselves into paramilitary units and marched on the coke works on March 30. Frick had anticipated this possibility, and private police and the sheriff's deputies defended the works; the resulting confrontation left at least seven strikers dead and many others wounded. Hearing what happened, Carnegie sent Frick a letter suggesting that the latter contact Pennsylvania Governor Robert Pattison and request National Guard troops, which Frick did.

The troops were quickly dispatched. On April 2, they repelled a force of between 400 and 700 striking miners, leaving nine dead and many more wounded. Additional troops arrived to quell the violence, and Frick supplemented his force with Pinkertons. Eventually, the strike degenerated into a cycle of violence that lasted nearly two months. On May 21, the UMWA called for an end to the strike. While the UMWA could not prevent Frick and Carnegie from imposing the sliding scale (essentially wage cuts) and the nine-hour shift, it did win a victory of sorts considering that the industrialists had failed to break the union.[27] In the end, both sides declared victory, though neither got exactly what it had wanted, an outcome reminiscent of the resolution at Homestead two years before.

There was one last bit of labor trouble facing Carnegie in 1891. Hot on the heels of the trouble at Edgar Thomson and H. C. Frick & Company, the skilled workers at the recently purchased Duquesne Steel quit their jobs and refused to return until the company raised their wages. Specifically, Duquesne's workers wanted the same wage scale being paid in Carnegie's other mills (specifically, Homestead). Frick hired men to pose as workers at Duquesne to identify the "troublemakers" among the work's remaining employees (i.e., men who advocated unionization). Once his spies identified the leaders of the nascent strike, Frick fired them immediately and then wrote to his superintendents at Edgar Thomson and Homestead, demanding that the men not be hired there, essentially blackballing them from the iron and steel industry. Moreover, Frick requested that the sheriff dispatch deputies to the works to defend it against the striking workers and to protect the scab laborers he planned to import. The presence of the deputies dissuaded the other workers from going on strike, as did the AAISW's refusal to endorse sympathy strikes at any of the company's other mills. The swift use of company spies, hard-handed tactics, and sheriff's deputies brought the strike to a swift end on terms unfavorable to the workers. These events proved Carnegie's assertion in his autobiography that "labor is usually helpless against capital," and perfectly illustrate how vindictive he and Frick could be when it came to their men.[28]

As this chapter demonstrates, Carnegie and Frick had a long history of tense relations with their employees in the years leading up to the Homestead strike. However, both men had much to celebrate on New Year's Day, 1892: all in all, 1891 was a banner year for them. While nation-wide the production of crude steel had declined by more than 14 percent, Carnegie's plants had increased production by nearly 21 percent, increasing the two Carnegie companies' (Carnegie, Phipps & Company and Carnegie Brothers & Company) share of the steel market by an astonishing 33 percent.[29] Moreover, Carnegie and Frick had successfully put down three strikes and largely broke the unions in their mills. Though they sometimes differed on timing and even on specific tactics, they remained thoroughly committed to the same goal: de-unionizing their companies' works.

However, there still existed one problem, an issue exposed by the trouble at Duquesne: the AAISW at Homestead provided a bad example to the workers at Carnegie's other plants because of the AAISW's seemingly successful challenge to management in 1889. Carnegie himself had once remarked that a company could not be both union and non-union, and the events at Duquesne in the summer of 1891 seemed to prove him right. Unhappy since the summer of 1889, both he and Frick agreed that the AAISW had to be forced out at Homestead, and they planned to use the upcoming contract negotiations in 1892 to do just that.

NOTES

1   Melvyn Dubofsky, *The State and Labor in Modern America* (Chapel Hill, NC: University of North Carolina Press, 1994), 2.

2   Andrew Carnegie, "An Employer's View of the Labor Question," in *The Andrew Carnegie Reader*, Ed. Joseph Frazier Wall (Pittsburgh, PA: University of Pittsburgh Press, 1992), 96.

3   David Brody, *Steelworkers in America: The Nonunion Era* (New York: Harper Torchbooks, 1960), 50.

4   Jonathan Rees, "Homestead in Context: Andrew Carnegie and the Decline of the Amalgamated Association of Iron and Steel Workers," *Pennsylvania History* vol. 64 no. 4 (Autumn, 1997), 509–513.

5   Ibid., 520.

6   Brody, *Steelworkers in America*, 5.

7   Rees, "Homestead in Context," 509–515.

8   Brody, *Steelworkers in America*, 2, 44–45; and H. W. Brands, *The Reckless Decade: America in the 1890s* (Chicago, IL: University of Chicago Press, 2002), 60.

9   Joshua L. Rosenbloom, "Strikebreaking and the Labor Market in the United States, 1881–1894," *The Journal of Economic History*, 187.

10   Peter Krass, *Carnegie* (Hoboken, NJ: John Wiley & Sons, 2002), 212.

11   Andrew Carnegie, *Autobiography of Andrew Carnegie* (New York, NY: Houghton Mifflin, 1929), 228.

12   James H. Bridge, *A Romance of Millions: The Inside History of the Carnegie Steel Company* (New York, NY: Aldine, 1903), 185–186; Paul Krause, *The Battle for Homestead, 1880–1892: Politics, Culture, and Steel* (Pittsburgh, PA: University of Pittsburgh Press, 1992); and Quentin R. Skrabec, Jr., *Henry Clay Frick: The Life of the Perfect Capitalist* (Jefferson, NC: McFarland, 2010), 58–59.

13   David Nasaw, *Andrew Carnegie* (New York, NY: The Penguin Press, 2006); and Krass, *Carnegie*, 209-210.

14   Skrabec, *Henry Clay Frick*, 86; and Krass, *Carnegie*, 213.

15   Samuel A. Schreiner, *Henry Clay Frick: The Gospel of Greed* (New York, NY: St. Martin's, 1995), 50; and Skrabec, *Henry Clay Frick*, 221.

16   Schreiner, *Henry Clay Frick*, 50; and Krass, *Carnegie*, 222.

17   Les Standiford, *Meet You in Hell* (New York: Crown, 2005), 80.

18   Carnegie, "An Employer's View of the Labor Question," 99.

19   Schreiner, *Henry Clay Frick*, 65.

20   Standiford, *Meet You in Hell*, 101.

21   In Joseph Frazier Wall, *Andrew Carnegie* (Pittsburgh, PA: University of Pittsburgh Press, 1989), 528–530.

22   Brands, *The Reckless Decade*, 130.

23   Krass, *Carnegie*, 271.

24   Ibid., 270–274; and Nasaw, *Andrew Carnegie*, 390.

25   Schreiner, *Henry Clay Frick*, 55.

26   Skrabec, *Henry Clay Frick*, 110; and Nasaw, *Andrew Carnegie*, 390.

27   Nasaw, *Andrew Carnegie*, 392.

28   Carnegie, *Autobiography of Andrew Carnegie*, 243. Quoted in Nasaw, *Andrew Carnegie*, 394.

29   Kenneth Warren, *Triumphant Capitalism: Henry Clay Frick and the Industrial Transformation of Industrial America* (Pittsburgh, PA: University of Pittsburgh Press, 1996), 75.

CHAPTER 4

The Lockout and Strike

The first European inhabitant of what became Homestead is believed to have been German immigrant Sebastian Frederick, who settled there in the 1770s. Frederick claimed 303 acres extending from the bank of the Monongahela River to the town's present-day cemetery. Frederick was a squatter, meaning that he did not own the land, and he supported himself mainly through hunting, fishing, and trapping. At some point during or immediately after the American War of Independence, he moved on (whether by his choice or because he was forced out is unknown) and disappeared from the historical record. In 1786, a farmer and trader named John McClure who had moved to the region from Carlisle in 1760 purchased the land. He bought approximately 330 acres extending along the Monongahela River between present-day Amity Street and Munhall Hollow. His son (also named John) inherited the land when McClure died in 1811; when the younger John McClure died in 1833, the land was divided among his eight sons. The youngest, Abdiel (only 17 at the time), received the westernmost portion of the land. Over the next few decades, Abdiel sold small portions of the land, which encouraged a modest amount of development. Yet, even as late as the 1860s, the area that came to be known as Homestead (after "Amity Homestead," the name John McClure Sr. bestowed on the land) remained a bucolic paradise of small family farms.

That began changing in the early 1870s. In 1872, Abdiel formed the Homestead Bank and Insurance Company with another local landowner, Lowry H. West. Abdiel immediately sold 113 acres to the company, which in turn subdivided the land into plots. The plan was to sell the land to wealthy and middle-class Pittsburghers looking to escape the soot and stench that accompanied the city's booming industrial growth, and the three-day sale netted more than $385,000 on 447 lots. The plots' new

One of the first plants built in Homestead was a glass factory owned by Bryce, Higbee & Company, which opened in 1879.

owners quickly built houses, and by the following year, the town had been linked by railroad with Pittsburgh. The small boom stopped with the Panic of 1873, which froze credit and wiped out the savings of many of the very people who were building their suburban retreats in Homestead. Consequently, a decade after the initial land sale, the town boasted only 600 residents.

The depression forced down the price of land, which changed the town's character by encouraging industrial development and the immigration of factory laborers to Homestead, who nearly doubled the town's anemic population but changed its character: small working-class houses, gambling houses, brothels, and taverns elbowed out bucolic suburban retreats for the privileged.[1]

Eventually, the town's industrial development would encourage two large waves of immigration. First, during the 1870s and 1880s, came the British, Irish, and Germans. These were followed by large groups of Eastern and Southern Europeans (Poles, Slavs, Russians, and Italians) in the late 1880s and 1890s. This second wave was often imported as strikebreakers against the "old" immigrants, so there was some lingering ethnic animosity that capitalists such as Carnegie and Frick exploited rather effectively.[2] Within a decade, Homestead had transformed from a retreat for the privileged into a working-class factory town.

A more important development was the construction of the Homestead steelworks in 1879. A consortium of local iron-makers under the name Pittsburgh Bessemer Steel Company built the works, and it quickly earned a reputation for being one of the most technologically advanced steel mills in the United States. Under the authoritarian management of William Clark (owner of the Solar Iron Works), Homestead first rolled steel rails in August 1881, and soon the company was turning out 200 tons of steel per day and had secured lucrative contracts for 15,000 tons of steel.[3] Unfortunately for the Pittsburgh Bessemer Steel Company, Clark was not a skilled labor negotiator, and he caused at least five serious confrontations with the works' laborers over the next two years. Clark initially tried to set wages below the prevailing rate in nearby Pittsburgh. Over the following five months, his skilled workers responded by disrupting production through slowdowns and shutdowns. Management and labor were often in conflict; early on, a confrontation between strikers and strikebreakers was broken up by deputy sheriffs and resulted in at least one death.

Management blamed the Amalgamated Association of Iron and Steelworkers (AAISW) for the generally unproductive relationship between labor and management. In an attempt to break the union, on New Year's Day, 1882, Clark demanded his workers sign contracts not to strike or join the AAISW; those who were already members had to resign. Most of Homestead's workers refused, so Clark locked them out and shut down the works. The workers organized themselves and, for the next two months, prevented scabs from entering the Homestead works. Having no rails to supply its customers, the Pittsburgh Bessemer Steel Company began defaulting on orders and was therefore unable to secure new ones. In March, Clark was forced to accede to the AAISW's demands, and the workers returned to work. Clark resigned as Homestead's manager and left the town, never to return.[4] Yet, this move hardly brought peace. Homestead's workers went out on strike again in June, the beginning of a four-month strike that left the Pittsburgh Bessemer Steel Company unable to fill its orders.

The workers' discontent, coupled with a rapid dip in the price of steel (which left the company short of capital), convinced some of the Pittsburgh Bessemer Steel Company's stockholders that the company and its works were a bad investment. A group of the company's stockholders pooled their shares and approached Carnegie about purchasing the stock. This offer came at a fortuitous time for Carnegie: though the market for steel had declined in the preceding months, the demand for his product far outpaced what his mills could generate. Purchasing Homestead would allow him to meet the demand for steel and, at the same time, remove a potential rival from the local steel market before prices improved. He created a new company (Carnegie, Phipps & Company) and purchased the shareholders' stock in the Homestead works, paying them with notes that were redeemed using the profits generated by Homestead; in other words, the Homestead works cost him little out of pocket.

At the time of Carnegie's purchase, the Homestead works housed six powerful AAISW lodges, each representing the works' different "departments" and accounting for more than one-fifth of the works' employees. The lodges were well organized and had, in the recent past, successfully forced the plant's previous ownership to meet their demands. Despite these potential obstacles, Carnegie was very pleased with his acquisition of the works, which vastly expanded his capacity. Though Homestead was one of the best-equipped and most modern steel plants in the country (and perhaps the world), one of the first things Carnegie did at Homestead was build two new mills: one to construct structure shapes (beams, girders, etc.) and another to build steel plates that could be used as armor for America's growing Navy. Both were an attempt to get out of the steel rail market, which was in decline.

Over the next seven years, Carnegie spent $3 million in technological upgrades designed to increase the works' profitability by cutting the employees' pay by 17 percent.[5] The most important upgrade by far was the construction of the country's first commercially successful open-hearth furnaces in 1886, which allowed the works to turn out a substantial amount of armor for the U.S. Navy. The steady drumbeat of orders gradually increased the size of Homestead's workforce from 1,600 to approximately 4,000 by the spring of 1892, and the works swelled to become the largest and most technologically advanced in the country. It sprawled across 90 acres and housed a converting department containing two Bessemer furnaces, a finishing mill, and a blooming mill, as well as four open-hearth furnaces. Though the Edgar Thomson works eclipsed Homestead in monthly output, the Homestead works nonetheless ranked in the top five most productive mills in the United States at that time.[6]

One consequence was that the town of Homestead, which had only 2,000 residents in 1880, increased in population by 600 percent over the next 12 years, and many of those residents relied directly or indirectly on the steelworks for their livelihoods. The company even acted as a bank, taking deposits from its employees and providing them with mortgages. The town burgess (equivalent to mayor) was even a steelworker (and AAISW member) named "Honest" John McLuckie, who was well respected in Homestead, having won his office in 1890 in a four-way race 811 votes to 5.[7] In other words, Homestead's citizenry was heavily dependent on the steel mill and the company, a fact that decisively shaped the lockout out and its legacy.

After the confrontation with the AAISW in 1889 (chronicled in Chapter 3), both Carnegie and Frick had waited restlessly for the company's contract with its workers at Homestead to expire on June 30, 1892. They considered the works a bad example to Carnegie's other plants and believed that unionism would reappear at all of the company's works unless decisive action was taken against the AAISW at Homestead. In addition, the eyes of the iron and steel industry were on Homestead. Would the company blink as it had in 1889, or would Frick stand strong against the union? Committed to rolling back wages and permanently break the AAISW, Frick knew the stakes were high and was determined to reassert control over the mill. At the same time, the AAISW looked forward to the contract negotiations because winning concessions from Frick (known as one of the toughest, most anti-labor men in the industry) would strengthen the union's hand in dealing with other mills. Moreover, union leaders were confident that, given the surge in the union's strength, they could maintain the favorable terms of the 1889 contract. In other words, both sides had quite a bit at stake in the summer of 1892, and each had every reason to expect victory.

Election of 1892

The election of 1892 pitted incumbent Republican president Benjamin Harrison against the Democratic former president Grover Cleveland (the only man to serve two nonconsecutive terms as president). Harrison had become president after defeating Cleveland in a close and extremely controversial election four years before. In the presidential election of 1888, incumbent Cleveland had won the popular vote (48.6 percent to 47.8 percent) but lost in the Electoral College (168 votes to Harrison's 233), a situation that has only occurred four times in the nation's history. Not surprisingly, this left the Democrats feeling extremely embittered and led to a hard-fought rematch in the presidential election of 1892.

One of the most important issues during the election of 1892 revolved around the Tariff Act of 1890 (known at the time as the McKinley Tariff after its primary supporter, Republican congressman William McKinley). Though the bill lowered or eliminated some tariffs on some products (sugar, tea, and coffee are good examples), in general the McKinley Tariff raised the average import duties (taxes paid on imports) from 38 percent to a whopping 49.5 percent. This is called "protectionism," and the goal was to "protect" American industries by raising the price of imports and thus providing a price incentive for consumers to buy products made in the United States; as such, American industrialists such as Andrew Carnegie and Henry Clay Frick heavily supported tariffs in general and the McKinley Tariff in particular.

Democrats opposed tariffs because they made goods more expensive for consumers and discouraged competition (by artificially raising the price of imports, domestic businesses had no incentive to find ways to improve their efficiency and lower their costs). While Cleveland did not oppose *all* tariffs, he did oppose the McKinley Tariff and called for a reduction in the average import duty. In addition, Cleveland adopted some traditionally Republican policies (specifically, he attacked the coinage of silver and the issuance of paper money) and was therefore seen as a Democrat that industrialists could "do business with."

The entry of a third-party candidate, the Populist Party's James B. Weaver, likely cost Cleveland some votes, but the Democratic former president again beat Harrison in the popular vote, 46 percent to 43 percent, a difference of approximately 381,000 votes. Cleveland's victory in the Electoral College was even bigger, 277 votes to Harrison's 145 and Weaver's 4, and Cleveland returned to the White House.

Another important consideration was that 1892 was an election year. The presidential contest, a rematch between incumbent Benjamin Harrison and challenger Grover Cleveland, was a replay of the incredibly close presidential election four years earlier. In 1888, Democrat Grover Cleveland had been defeated in his bid for re-election by Harrison, who managed to win the White House in the Electoral College after losing the popular vote by a little over one percentage point. Both sides expected this election to be just as close, and the Republicans were extremely concerned that a protracted strike at Homestead could galvanize Democrats and shift the election. The union's leadership was confident that the Republicans would pressure Carnegie and Frick to settle the dispute as quickly and quietly as possible, and they were correct: as early as July 2, President Harrison had met with a prominent Pennsylvania Republican and instructed him to convince Frick to settle the strike before it influenced the election. Harrison implied, and may have even said outright, that an unfavorable response would lead him to seriously review all federal patronage dollars flowing into Pennsylvania.[8] As the crisis developed, it became clear that Democratic newspapers successfully stoked anger over the events at Homestead and directed it toward the Republican Party. In addition, the Navy was shocked that Carnegie and Frick would allow a work shutdown to happen in the first place and then deal with it (from the Navy's perspective) so ineptly; after all, the United States Navy was an important customer, and a protracted work stoppage such as this might imperil future Navy contracts.[9]

Thus, on the surface, the AAISW's leadership had every reason to feel confident, but they had badly overestimated the strength of their bargaining position and had drawn the wrong lessons from their previous dealings with the company. The AAISW's leadership had assumed that Carnegie's fear of defaulting on the armor contract with the Navy would make him unwilling to allow a long work stoppage, and this would therefore encourage him to restrain Frick. In fact, Carnegie and Frick had planned for this and begun stockpiling armor in the event of a strike or lockout. What made stockpiling possible was the steel market slowing down in 1892. With the constant technological upgrades at Homestead, production at the plant was vastly exceeding demand. In other words, a work stoppage was actually *beneficial* to Carnegie because otherwise the company would simply keep producing steel for which there would be few buyers.[10]

Finally, and importantly, the company's management had been reshuffled in the wake of the 1889 strike, which was part of a larger process of consolidation designed to bring Carnegie's sprawling iron and steel empire under the umbrella of a single company. This was a complex process that took years to accomplish, but, at exactly the same time the company's contract was due to expire, the process was achieved. Carnegie's two main steel companies—Carnegie Brothers & Company and Carnegie, Phipps & Company—became Carnegie Steel Company on July 1, 1892. It was the largest steel company in the world, and serving as its chairman was Henry Clay Frick. One of the most notoriously anti-union men in the history of American business was in charge, and he had the full and unqualified support of Andrew Carnegie when it came to breaking the AAISW. Moreover, Frick had been chosen precisely because of his reputation as a ruthless strikebreaker—the "prince of coke" was chosen specifically because he would not negotiate. This was a fight to the death that Frick had every intention of winning.

One of the important goals behind consolidating Carnegie's companies was to standardize wage rates across the mills. Up to this point, wage rates for steelworkers varied across works, even those owned by the same company. This was, in part, due to the different machinery available at the various works, which heavily governed the amount of steel each worker could produce during a shift, but the differences in pay also reflected the relative strength of each works' union lodges. Naturally, employees at the various works knew about the differences in pay, which only encouraged workers at lower-paying works to agitate for raises. By consolidating the companies, Frick and Carnegie hoped to standardize pay by bring the higher-paying works (such as Homestead) in line with the lower wages paid at the company's other works. Of course, the key to achieving this goal was breaking the union at Homestead because the AAISW was a serious impediment to any attempt to lower the workers' wages.

In January 1891 (a full 18 months before the contract at Homestead was due to expire), Frick approached the *National Labor Tribune*'s editor, former steel roller and previous vice president of the American Federation of Labor (AFL), William Martin, to gather and compile information about prevailing wages in the iron and steel industry from across the nation. The numbers indicated that the wages paid at Homestead were higher than the national average, a point that Carnegie and Frick hoped to use in the public relations battle with the union (they did not, however, plan on mentioning that workers at Homestead were also much more productive per employee than workers at Edgar Thomson or Duquesne). A somewhat conservative man, Martin had resigned from both the AAISW and the AFL, and, in July 1891, he received a well-paid position on Carnegie's staff, where he set about formulating a new wage scale to bring Homestead's workers in line with the employees at Carnegie's non-union mills.[11]

In January 1892, John Potter, Abbott's replacement as Homestead's superintendent, requested that the AAISW propose a contract to govern four of the plant's 10 departments (the other six were receiving technological upgrades and would be negotiated later, Potter explained). The union suggested renewing the terms of the 1889 contract: the tonnage rate would remain the same, the floor below which wages on the sliding scale would not fall would stay at $25 per ton, and the contract would be for three years, expiring on June 30, 1895. When the union's leadership presented Potter with their proposal early the following month, he rejected their terms and offered instead the wage scale that Martin had developed the previous year, which was clearly unacceptable to the union. Martin's plan called for wage reductions in these four departments (affecting about 325 of the plant's 3,800 workers) by dropping the sliding scale wages' floor to $22 per ton and by lowering the tonnage rate by 15 percent. In addition, the company reserved the right to reduce other skilled workers' wages if the company introduced cost-cutting methods or new machinery. Given that Carnegie was constantly installing new machines and developing labor-saving techniques, this clause meant that wages for any of the remaining skilled workers would almost surely be reduced at a later date. In addition to deep wage cuts, the contract would have severely weakened the union's bargaining position in future negotiations. The union leaders left the meeting without scheduling another.[12]

After Homestead turned into a full-fledged public relations disaster for the Carnegie Steel Company, Carnegie tried to place the blame squarely on Frick's shoulders, but the record shows that he was as aggressive in confronting the union as Frick. Though Carnegie took an extended summer vacation in Europe (as was his habit) in the summer of 1892, he was totally engaged with the situation at Homestead in the months leading up to the contract's expiration. For instance, in early April, he prepared and sent a notice that he ordered Frick to post at Homestead; though this never occurred, the notice provides insight into Carnegie's character. The notice read:

> These Works having been consolidated with the Edgar Thomson and Duquesne and other mills, there has been forced upon this firm question whether its Works are to be run "Union" or "Non-Union." As the vast majority of our employees are Non-Union, the Firm has decided that the minority must give place to the majority. These works therefore will be necessarily Non-Union after the expiration of the present agreement.
>
> This does not imply that the men will take lower wages. On the contrary, most of the men at Edgar Thomson and Duquesne Works, both Non-Union, have made and are making higher wages than those at Homestead which has hitherto been Union.
>
> [. . .]
>
> A scale will be arranged which will compare favorably with that at the other works named; that is to say, the Firm intends that the men of Homestead shall make as much as the men at either Duquesne or Edgar Thomson. Owing to the great changes and improvements made in the Converting Works, Beam Mills, Open Hearth Furnaces, etc. [. . .] the product of the works will be

greatly increased, so that at the rates per ton paid at Braddock and Duquesne, the monthly earnings of the men may be greater than hitherto. While the number of men will, of course, be reduced, the extensions at Duquesne and Edgar Thomson as well as at Homestead will, it is hoped, enable the firm to give profitable employment to such of its desirable employees as may be temporarily displaced. [. . .]

This action is not taken in any spirit of hostility to labor organizations, but every man must see that the firm cannot run Union and Non-Union. It must be one or the other.

The notice was vintage Carnegie: disingenuous and dishonest. In it, Carnegie asserts as fact that a company "cannot run Union and Non-Union" and that the question of whether to be a union or a non-union company had been "forced" upon the Carnegie Steel Company. It was not the first time that he used this line of reasoning; in the lead-up to previous labor disputes, he had blamed the mill's workers for "allowing" his competitors to pay lower wages than he did, thus "forcing" him to lower wages to remain competitive. This statement was about preserving Carnegie's public image of being a "friend of labor" by presenting de-unionization as something that he was "forced" to do. Surely, if the men at Edgar Thomson and other Carnegie plants had been given the choice, they would have opted to be unionized; after all, the only reason these works were not unionized was because Frick and Carnegie had done everything in their power to uproot the mills' union lodges.

Clearly, remaining competitive was not the issue: breaking the AAISW at Homestead was. Despite what Carnegie said in public, he and Frick had decided to destroy the AAISW years before and had carefully planned their strategy, which involved shifting the "blame" to the AAISW. In addition, Carnegie asserted "that the minority must give place to the majority," as if the wage rates had been decided by the workers through a vote and he was simply acceding to the majority's wishes. This was the same strategy Carnegie adopted in justifying his decision to pursue naval armor contracts. As Chapter 3 demonstrates, the majority of Carnegie's workers were non-union because he and Frick had spent the last few years ruthlessly union-busting the company's mills.

That breaking the AAISW at Homestead would yield higher wages for the workers was probably the most damning assertion in the notice. Carnegie asserted (questionably) that wages were higher at Duquesne and Edgar Thomson and implied this was because those mills were non-union. Therefore, according to Carnegie, the workers at Homestead should welcome the transformation to a non-union shop because "[. . .] the Firm intends that the men of Homestead shall make as much as the men at either Duquesne or Edgar Thomson," implying the impediment to higher wages was the AAISW. In reality, Carnegie and Frick's goal was to both cut the mill's workforce *and* lower the remaining workers' wages, a conclusion supported by the contract that they offered to the union's leadership in March.

Along with this notice, Carnegie sent a personal note to Frick that directed him to close the plant rather than negotiate with the workers, which was his preferred tactic in labor disputes. Frick elected not to post the notice, fearing that it would immediately lead to a strike that would result in another public relations debacle. Instead, he proposed offering contract terms that the AAISW simply could not accept and then refusing to negotiate with the union (another tactic he used with great effect in other labor disputes). This strategy would ensure that the company was not blamed for the work stoppage and would give Frick a freer hand in hiring scab labor. In May, while vacationing in England, Carnegie sent Frick a note that assented to Frick's plan. Carnegie wrote:

> [. . .] your reputation will shorten [a strike], so that I do not believe it will be much of a struggle. [The company's board of directors] all approve of anything you do, *not stopping short of approval of a contest. We are with you to the end.*[13]

On June 10, less than a month before the contract expired, Carnegie sent Frick another letter in which he reiterated that Frick should not negotiate with the workers.[14]

As the months ticked by toward the end of the contract, the union tried to negotiate with Frick, but he refused to deviate from his position: the agreement was "take it or leave it," and the deadline was June 24. In a move designed to make an offer that the AAISW simply could not accept, Frick demanded that the new contract expire on December 31, 1894, because strikes were harder to sustain during winter months. Frick (undoubtedly hoping to aggravate the situation) ordered Potter to notify the AAISW that if the union did not agree to his terms by June 24, the company would begin negotiating with the men as individuals, essentially breaking the union. On June 23, the union refused to accede to Frick's demands.

Once the new deadline passed, the company became more provocative. For instance, on June 25, a notice appeared at the Homestead works announcing that, henceforth, the management would no longer deal with the AAISW, only with individual workers. More ominous was the fact that the company had begun reinforcing the works by building 11-foot-high fences topped with 18 inches of barbed wire and punctuated with a series of holes just large enough for the barrel of a gun. At the barricade's entrance were enormous searchlights and fire hydrants capable of producing enormously powerful water sprays.[15] In other words, the Homestead works were transformed into an imposing stronghold that locals quickly dubbed "Fort Frick."

This was an aggressive move on Frick's part, and the workers responded in kind. Some of the workers hanged effigies of Frick and Homestead superintendent Potter on company property. In addition, in a meeting at the Homestead opera house on the morning of June 29, most of the works' employees (including non-AAISW members) registered their support for the advisory committee's decision to reject Frick's terms. The message was not lost on Frick, and he began shutting down various departments at the works, a process that was completed on June 30. The lockout had begun, and Frick and Carnegie had gotten the labor stoppage they wanted.

With tensions running high, rumors swept through the town. During the AAISW meeting on June 30 to discuss the company's final offer, one man claimed that he had heard the company was importing 300 scab workers from Philadelphia, a claim that inflamed the crowd. The union's executive committee realized that they needed to keep control of the men to win the public relations battle and to mount an effective defense against the company's scab laborers. Following the meeting at the opera house, they formed an advisory committee that included Burgess John L. McLuckie (a steelworker and union member), Hugh O'Donnell (a steel roller and union member), and representatives from the AAISW's eight Homestead lodges. Essentially, this meant that there was little difference between Homestead's town government and the local lodges of the AAISW, so the fight with Carnegie Steel would include not just the workers, but the entire town as well.

Recognizing that Carnegie and Frick would most likely try to import scab laborers protected by Pinkerton guards, the advisory committee created subcommittees charged with patrolling the river and various points of interest (entrances to the town, the rail lines leading into Homestead, the works, etc.). These subcommittees quickly took on a paramilitary character: thousands of striking workers were divided into three "divisions," headed by eight "captains," who were in turn overseen by a "commander." Each division was made responsible for an eight-hour shift, and the goal was to create an infrastructure so responsive that the advisory committee members would receive up-to-the-minute intelligence from a dragnet that covered a five-mile radius.[16] A giant steam whistle was installed at the town's electric light system so that Homestead's inhabitants

Figure 4.1 The Homestead works, circa 1892. This is where the Pinkteron agents attempted to land and where they were later forced to "walk the gauntlet" after surrendering.

Courtesy of Rivers of Steel National Heritage Area.

could be quickly summoned if (as expected) the company tried to reopen the steelworks with scab labor. The advisory committee even went so far as to secure a small steamboat (the *Edna*) for patrolling the river. Knowing that any action taken by the workers would be heavily reported and scrutinized by the general public, the advisory committee took steps to present the best possible face to the world: members of various subcommittees visited Homestead's saloons and "requested" that the owners take action against drunkenness or rowdy behavior. In addition, the advisory committee removed the various effigies of Frick and other company officials that had appeared all over town. In other words, the AAISW took definitive steps to prepare for what seemed like an inevitable showdown between Carnegie Steel and the union.

Behind the scenes, Carnegie and Frick had also prepared for the work stoppage that they had made inevitable. Beyond surrounding the works with a fence, Frick moved to acquire replacement workers and private security to protect them.

Following the works' shutdown at the end of June, many of Homestead's middle managers left town. They claimed they were going on vacation since there was no work to be done, but rumors swirled through Homestead that Carnegie and Frick had dispatched them across the northeast to obtain replacement workers. On June 25 (the same day the company announced that it would no longer deal with the AAISW), Frick

> In early June, weeks before the contract with the AAISW expired, Carnegie instructed his cousin Dod to head to Britain and begin recruiting English and Scottish scab labor in anticipation of a work stoppage at Homestead.

wrote to Robert Pinkerton (son of Allan and one of the Pinkerton National Detective Agency's managers) and requested 300 Pinkertons to serve as guards for the works beginning on July 6. On June 26, Carnegie Steel's lawyer, Philander C. Knox, acting under Frick's orders, met with Allegheny County Sheriff William H. McCleary (who replaced McCandless in 1890). During this meeting, Knox informed the Sheriff of the company's plans to hire Pinkertons to protect the Homestead works, and he asked McCleary to deputize the agents; McCleary refused.

As June 30 (the last day of the contract between the AAISW and the company) approached, local newspapers editorialized about Frick's obdurate behavior and speculated that he was trying to foment a strike, which would give him the excuse he needed to replace the entire workforce at Homestead. For Frick, this was never about saving money on wages (though that was certainly an added bonus); the total savings generated by the wage cuts he proposed worked out to about $0.02 per ton of steel (in an era when the company was getting between $30 and $35 dollars a ton), or about $20,000, a minuscule fraction of the company's annual profits.[17]

There is no doubt that Carnegie and Frick both expected and welcomed a confrontation with their employees at Homestead. Frick and Carnegie had offered the AAISW a contract that it simply could not accept and then deliberately tried provoking the union by demanding that it agree to their terms a week before the old contract expired. After the strike began, Frick's provocations increased. On July 2, the company's secretary issued a statement to the effect that the company would spare no expense to ensure that the Homestead works would henceforth be operated as a non-union plant. Ominously, the company also announced the plant was currently closed for repairs and would reopen in two or three weeks. At that time, any workers who did not return to their positions would be replaced. Burgess McLuckie struck back the following day, saying that the strikers would not allow Carnegie and Frick to "bulldoze" them, and he asserted, "They have never imported a man into Homestead [and] they never will. We will not permit it."[18] The time for negotiation had passed, and everyone knew it; reporters flocked to town to cover what everyone expected to be an explosive confrontation. The *Pittsburgh Post* said it all with the headline "IT LOOKS LIKE WAR."[19]

On July 4, Frick went through the motions of formally requesting Sheriff McCleary to secure the Homestead works so that he could reopen the mills with scab labor. After confirming with Robert Pinkerton that Pinkerton agents were en route, Frick wrote to Carnegie and laid out, in detail, what would happen over the next few days. According to his note, Frick planned to land the Pinkertons at Homestead early on the morning of July 6. Frick expected that the 300 private police would easily take over the Homestead works and open it with new workers in a few days. In response to Frick's request for help with recovering the works, Sheriff McCleary, accompanied by former sheriffs Samuel B. Cluely and Joseph H. Gray (now the deputy sheriff), traveled to Homestead on the morning of July 5 and met with the advisory committee at about 10:00 a.m. The advisory committee offered to provide whatever men were necessary to protect the works and was even willing to post $10,000 for each man that McCleary deputized, but the sheriff refused. After touring the works, McCleary admitted that he saw no evidence of vandalism or disorder, but he nonetheless informed the advisory committee of his intention to return the works to Carnegie Steel. At this point, Hugh O'Donnell asked McCleary if this was all he had to say, and McCleary indicated it was. Following a lengthy recess during which the advisory committee met in private, O'Donnell declared the advisory committee was dissolved and its members would accept no responsibility for "[. . .] any disorder or lawless acts, either in Homestead Borough or Mifflin Township."[20]

Asking the sheriffs to serve as their witnesses, the advisory committee members removed their lapel badges and placed them on a nearby table. Next, the members burned the advisory committee's minutes. This was an important public relations move (it was witnessed by at least one reporter) in the never-ending struggle to secure favorable press coverage and put the blame for any violence on Carnegie and Frick. In practice, the advisory committee's members would continue to play an important leadership role as events unfolded over the next few days, and Frick would do his best to hold them legally responsible for the violence. After witnessing the dissolution of the advisory committee, McCleary left Homestead at about 2:00 p.m. without having taken control of the works. Though the advisory committee and townspeople had been polite, the subtext was clear: any attempt to forcibly retake the works would be met with stiff resistance. McCleary reported what had happened to one of the company's attorneys, who in turn informed the sheriff about Frick's plans to use the Pinkertons to retake the works the following day. McCleary again refused the company's request (this time coming directly from Frick) to deputize the private police force, but the sheriff did dispatch Deputy Sheriff Gray to join the 300 Pinkertons on their barges when they tried to retake the works.[21]

At about 10:30 p.m. that evening, a train carrying 300 members of the Pinkerton National Detective agency arrived at Bellevue, Pennsylvania, a small town abutting the Ohio River about five miles west of Pittsburgh. Most of the men (about 260) were untrained recruits plucked off the streets of New York and Philadelphia; almost uniformly poor and desperate, they were lured by the promise of (pitiably low) wages and a uniform. Most had no idea what awaited them in Homestead. William B. Rodgers, the captain of the tugboat that pulled the Pinkertons' barges to Homestead, recalled, "the men talked freely of going to Carnegie's to act as watchmen and seemed to have no idea of being engaged in a work of danger."[22] This led John McLuckie to later characterize the confrontation as a battle

> [. . .] between laboring men because these Pinkertons and their associates were [. . .] there under pay, and the person who employed that force was safely placed away by the money he has wrung from the sweat of the men employed in that mill, employing in their stead workmen to go there and kill the men who made his money.[23]

Homestead superintendent Potter and Deputy Sheriff Gray were on hand to greet the Pinkertons and oversaw the transfer of the men onto two specially outfitted barges: the *Iron Mountain*, which was intended to serve as the men's barracks during their stay in Homestead, and the *Monongahela*, which was outfitted as a kitchen, dining room, and storage area. Once the men were safely loaded onto the barges, two tugboats—the *Little Bill* and the *Tide*—began transporting the barges to Homestead. After only a short time, however, the *Tide* was disabled, forcing the *Little Bill* to tow the two barges. On the trip downriver, the Pinkertons changed into their uniforms—a white shirt, slouched hat, and blue pants—and prepared for what many thought would be simple guard duty.

Unfortunately for the Pinkertons, the townspeople of Homestead used the delay between the beginning of the lockout and the arrival of the private police force to create an infrastructure capable of detecting such a development. A scout observed the barges as they approached the Smithfield Street Bridge and telegraphed the AAISW's headquarters in Homestead. By 2:30 a.m., the advisory committee was aware that Frick had made his move, and they began taking steps to neutralize it. To slow down and intimidate the Pinkertons, the AAISW launched the *Edna* to confront the *Iron Mountain* and the *Monongahela*. The *Edna* fired a few warning shots, a signal to the people of Homestead that the confrontation they had been expecting for a week had begun. As the *Iron Mountain* and the *Monongahela* passed by Homestead's shoreline, angry workers and their friends and family surrounded them. The large concentration of angry men and women turned to violence, and the advisory committee immediately lost whatever control it may have had over the crowd. Correspondents who witnessed the events firsthand described the confusion: there were shouts of "charge on them," and workers and townspeople alike rushed toward the shore, screaming at the barges. Shots were fired at the barges and tugboat, shattering windows and frightening the men inside. Trying to keep their men calm, Pinkerton captains Frederick Heinde and Charles Nordrum ordered the men to refrain from returning fire except in self-defense.[24]

At about 4:00 a.m., the steam whistle's shrill whine alerted Homestead's citizens that Carnegie Steel had made its move, and very quickly, men, women, and even some children began making their way to the works. Primed for violence by the harsh rhetoric emanating from both management and the union, they carried whatever weapons were handy, ranging from hunting rifles, shotguns, and pistols, to knives, boards, and even the occasional table leg. Angered by the company's attempt to retake the works by force, the crowd broke through a section of wall surrounding "Fort Frick" and advanced toward the company's wharf. By the time the barges reached the wharf at about 4:30 a.m., the Pinkertons had been under assault for more than an hour. Once the tugboat pushed the two barges to the riverbank, the crowd momentarily fell silent and the intermittent shooting ceased. The members of the advisory committee (Hugh O'Donnell in particular), aware that the press was watching them and would report their actions to the world, implored the townspeople not to fire on the Pinkertons, but they were swimming against the current. Anger overtook the crowd, whose members began screaming all manner of threats at the agents in the barges in the hope of persuading the Pinkertons to turn back. O'Donnell, trying to reassert control over the crowd, approached the barges and made an impassioned plea to the Pinkertons not to try to land, which he ended by imploring, "[. . .] in the name of God and humanity, don't attempt to land! Don't attempt to enter these works by force!"[25]

Following O'Donnell's plea, Captain Heinde stepped out onto the *Iron Mountain*'s deck and responded by saying that he and his men had been hired to retake the works, and that while the Pinkertons did not want bloodshed, they would fulfill their mission by force if necessary. O'Donnell, somewhat incredulously, replied, "I have no more to say. What you do here is at the risk of many lives. Before you enter those mills, you will trample over the dead bodies of three thousand honest working men."[26]

Despite O'Donnell's appeal, some of the Pinkertons tried lowering a gangplank to offload the men from the ship to the wharf. A group of workers approached the gangplank. A steelworker named William Foy threw himself on it and dared the men to walk "over my carcass." Heinde hit Foy in the head with a billy club and ordered his men to follow him onto the wharf. However, as he stepped onto the gangplank, Heinde somehow slipped on an oar, which went flying through the air and hit a worker in the face, knocking the surprised man to the ground. Another worker, perhaps mistaking the oar for having been thrown, rushed toward Heinde and hit him with a club, sending the Pinkerton captain to the ground. What happened next is a matter of some dispute. At least one, and possibly two, shots rang out, wounding both Foy and Heinde. Many of the newspaper correspondents (even those whose employers were sympathetic to Carnegie and Frick) claimed that it was a Pinkerton who fired the first shot, while Deputy Sheriff Gray, many of the Pinkertons, and even some of the workers argued that it was a worker who had fired first.

Regardless of who was responsible for firing the first shot, the result was electric. Another Pinkerton captain, J. W. Cooper, ordered his men to begin firing. They unleashed volley after volley of deadly rifle fire into the crowd. This only further enraged the crowd, for whom any sense of restraint had now disappeared; workers and townspeople unleashed their own furious volley of rifle, pistol, and musket fire. For 10 minutes, gunfire exploded along Homestead's riverbank: the Pinkertons firing from inside the barges, and the townspeople and workers firing from behind the makeshift barricades they had constructed in the days leading up to the imbroglio. Because of this, the total wounded (approximately two dozen) and killed either immediately or as a result of their wounds (about four) was relatively small, and the battle settled into a stalemate. The Pinkerton captains pressured Potter to let them try to offload again, but the superintendent refused, saying that he would not take responsibility for causing any more bloodshed.[27]

However, the firing gradually died down as it became clear to the strikers that the Pinkertons were cowed, at least for the moment; the force had retreated from the ships' decks and was now holed up inside the large cabins. According to historian Paul Krause, Potter mistakenly believed that the lull in fighting meant that the union's advisory committee had re-established control over the crowd, allowing the Pinkertons to land, take control of the works, and transport their wounded to a hospital in Pittsburgh.[28] If so, Potter was mistaken on two accounts: first, the advisory committee was not in control of the crowd; and second, even if it was, its members had no intention of allowing the Pinktertons into the works. Moreover, even as Potter and the Pinkertons were debating their next move, members of the advisory committee established an arsenal in a nearby building and had union members scouring the town in search of more weapons and ammunition that could be used to repel any attempt to land.[29] Furthermore, Potter was not in control of the Pinktertons, who were busy cutting firing holes into the barges' hulls to allow them to repel any attempt by the strikers to seize the ships. The strikers interpreted this development as a provocation and began looking for ways to sink the barges. Thus, even as a tense calm settled over Homestead at about 6:00 a.m., it was pregnant with the expectation of violence yet to come. However, the lull in fighting allowed the Pinkertons to load their wounded into the *Little Bill*, which took the men across the river so their wounds could be treated.

As news of the deadly encounter filtered out of Homestead, thousands of onlookers began gathering on the nearby hills to get a firsthand view of the carnage. Within two hours of the Pinkertons' attempt to land at Homestead, more than 5,000 people had gathered to watch the sporadic gunfire. More ominously, the standoff at Homestead had electrified Pittsburgh's working class, thousands of whom were arming themselves and making their way upstream to help repel the Pinkertons. Perhaps sensing that time was not on their side, at about 8:00 a.m., the Pinkertons made a second attempt to land and seize the steelworks. One of the Pinkerton captains announced to some nearby strikers his intention to disembark, which provoked a warning shot. The Pinkertons returned fire, killing four workers. These deaths seemed to enrage and unify the crowd, which represented a cross-section of the various ethnic groups that made up Homestead's workforce. The net result was to strengthen the strikers' commitment to keeping the works at all costs while at the same time eroding the Pinkertons' morale. Consequently, many of the Pinkertons (who were only in Homestead for the meager pay and were therefore hardly committed to the cause of seizing the works) refused to risk their lives trying to debark from the ships.

Yet, something had to be done. The barges were sitting ducks that offered little protection. For the next few hours, intermittent gunfire rang out, keeping the Pinkertons in their ships. Some of Homestead's inhabitants even commandeered two cannons (one of them from the town's Grand Army of the Republic lodge) and used them to fire on the *Iron Mountain* and the *Monongahela*.[30] Though many cannon balls missed the ships, a lucky shot had torn off one barge's roof, partially exposing the men inside, who began to panic. The untrained agents frantically searched for something to cover themselves from the gun and cannon fire, hiding under cots, tables, and even sacks of supplies. Many refused their superiors' orders, and the situation descended into chaos.

At about 11:00 a.m., the *Little Bill* returned to Homestead in an attempt to tow the *Iron Mountain* and the *Monongahela* away. The *Little Bill*'s reappearance provoked a furious volley of fire from the strikers that wounded a crew member and narrowly missed the tugboat's captain. The gunfire forced the *Little Bill*'s pilot from the wheelhouse, and the ship moved downstream away from the *Iron Mountain* and the *Monongahela*. By then, it had dawned on many of the Pinkertons that rescue, if it came at all, would not appear anytime soon, a terrifying prospect made worse by the strikers' concerted effort to sink the *Iron Mountain* and the *Monongahela*, which up to this point had offered some relative safety.

In an attempt to break the stalemate, the strikers set fire to a raft loaded with oil-soaked wood, which they launched in the direction of the *Iron Mountain* and the *Monongahela*. The Pinkertons could see the flaming raft floating toward them, inducing panic that was only contained when one of the captains threatened to shoot any man who tried to jump overboard. Fortunately, none of the men had to choose between burning to death or being shot, because the raft burned itself out before reaching either ship. The Pinkertons' relief was only momentary because the strikers next set fire to a railcar laden with barrels of oil, which they let run down the hill toward the wharf. This time, the Pinkertons were only spared when the car stopped on the wharf before reaching either ship. These efforts led to wilder schemes. The strikers also tried to dynamite the ships, which failed. They next poured oil into the water around the ships, trying to create a slick that they could then ignite. Clearly, the crowd would stop at nothing to prevent the Pinkertons from taking control of the works.

While these schemes to sink the barges failed, the strikers kept up a lethal volley of gunfire that claimed the life of one Pinkerton, Thomas Connors, who slowly bled to death from a wound in his right arm. The horror of Connors' death combined with the ongoing gun and cannon fire convinced many rank-and-file Pinkertons that they faced certain death if they did not surrender. The debate over surrender became so intense that one agent shot himself in the head rather than leave the ship.[31] While a small minority of agents argued that the strikers would kill them, the majority supported surrendering. Unfortunately for the Pinkertons, the crowd was in no mood to end the fighting. The Pinkertons tried to signal their surrender by raising a white flag, but the strikers shot the flag down at least twice. The crowd was enraged by the attempt to forcibly take the works and by the resulting deaths, and most were in no mood to compromise with Carnegie and Frick's small army of strikebreakers.

Moreover, a rumor was circulating through the crowd to the effect that the state militia was on its way, and the strikers were determined to exact the maximum punishment on the Pinkertons before it arrived.[32]

While these events unfolded at Homestead, another sort of battle raged in Pittsburgh. The violence at Homestead had forced Sheriff McCleary to meet with the city's political boss, Republican Christopher L. Magee, and his associate, William Flinn. Magee was a local millionaire who had gotten his start as an office boy at Park, McCurdy & Company, a Pittsburgh iron-making firm. Using his position as city treasurer, Magee had endeared himself to the city's industrialists by using public money to support local banks and financial markets. They repaid him by finding positions for Magee's supporters, creating a patronage network that kept Magee in office and ensured that men such as Carnegie and Frick would have a sympathetic ear and a helping hand in city hall. Flinn also served the city's industrial interests by simultaneously holding a state senate seat and serving on the executive committee of the Pennsylvania State Republican Party. Understandably concerned about the events at Homestead, none of these men were particularly inclined to see things from the strikers' perspective, though they did meet with the AAISW's national president, William Weihe, at about 9:00 a.m.

Weihe, a seven-foot-tall former iron-worker known to his men as "the Giant Puddler," requested that Sheriff McCleary contact Frick and get the Carnegie Steel chairman to meet with the strikers and settle the lockout/strike, if only to prevent further bloodshed. McCleary acquiesced to Weihe's request, but despite the morning's events, Frick took an even harder line against the union than before and flatly rejected the AAISW president's request to meet with the strikers. Shortly thereafter, the company's secretary issued a statement to the effect that the Homestead works were in Sheriff McCleary's hands and that McCleary had the authority to request National Guard troops. Perhaps mindful that the rest of the country was watching, Frick may have been trying to scapegoat McCleary; while the "prince of coke" cared little what people thought of him, he needed to tread carefully because he knew that Carnegie was very concerned about public perception. Frick, speaking to the press later that day, reinforced the point by asserting that the company could not "interfere" with any action that Sheriff McCleary would take.[33] Frick went even further, asserting that he had refused the AAISW's request to meet with the strikers even after one of the union's representatives (most likely Weihe) agreed to all of Frick's terms except changing the contract's expiration date from June 30 to December 30. Saying the matter was now in McCleary's hands, Frick claimed there was nothing left to negotiate. Frick even hinted that, should McCleary fail to secure the works, he fully

Governor Robert E. Pattison (1850–1904)

Robert E. Pattison was Pennsylvania's nineteenth governor. Pattison was born in Maryland, but his family moved to Philadelphia when he was five years old. His father, Robert Henry Pattison, was a Methodist Episcopalian minister. The future governor was educated in Philadelphia's public schools, including the city's famed Central High School.

Pattison studied law under the prominent Philadelphia politico Lewis C. Cassidy. Admitted to the city's bar in 1872 (at the age of 21), Pattison began a meteoric political rise: in 1877 he was elected Philadelphia's controller, a position to which he was re-elected in 1880. In this position, he was generally credited with saving the city from bankruptcy, which gave him credibility for a statewide run. In 1882, he was nominated by the Democratic Party to be the state's governor, and he was the first Democrat to win Pennsylvania's governorship since the Civil War. As governor, Pattison was somewhat inconsistent. For instance, he was among the first state officials to warn about the power of corporate monopolies but, at the same time, he used state power to restore control of the Homestead works to Carnegie and Frick. In addition, after promising not to appoint political bosses to statewide office, Pattison appointed his mentor, Lewis C. Cassidy, state attorney general.

Under the terms of Pennsylvania's constitution, governors could not serve two consecutive terms, so Pattison left office in 1887. While in private life, he served as president of Philadelphia's Chestnut Street National Bank and Trust Company. In 1890, the Democrats again nominated Pattison to be governor, and he won the election. After a tumultuous second term, which included the violence at Homestead, Pattison left office in 1895 and returned to his private law practice.

expected Pennsylvania Governor Robert Pattison to dispatch state militia to crush the strike.

In reality, Frick and Carnegie were hardly disappointed by Sheriff McCleary's failure to take the works, because it gave the company a freer hand to crush the AAISW once and for all. Carnegie and Frick had expected the sheriff to fail and reasoned that McCleary's inability to protect their property rights gave them an excuse to hire the Pinkertons; after all, who could argue with a property owner turning to a private police force after seemingly exhausting all other avenues of recovering his property? As Frick's public statements indicate, his and Carnegie's moves were calculated to provoke a strike and destroy the union, not to negotiate a contract that both management and labor could abide. Even after the AAISW's leadership agreed to nearly all of his conditions, Frick pressed on. Why win the battle when you can win the war?

Pattison was the youngest man in the nation's history to become a state governor.

At 10:00 a.m. on July 6, McCleary telegraphed his first appeal for state assistance in retaking the steelworks, claiming that the strikers numbered "at least" 5,000 and that "the civil authorities are utterly unable to cope with them."[34]

Unfortunately for Carnegie and Frick, Governor Pattison equivocated. Pattison, who was midway through his second term as governor, owed Magee a political debt. Though Pattison was a Democrat, Magee had sabotaged the candidacy of Republican George W. Delameter, an acolyte of Magee's nemesis, Senator Matthew S. Quay. Magee surely expected that Pattison would repay this political debt by quickly sending state militia troops to restore company control of the Homestead works. Pattison, however, saw the situation differently. He had won the governorship not only through Magee's political maneuverings, but also through the votes of Pennsylvania's workers, most of whom would take a dim view of any use of the state militia as strikebreakers. Pattison was therefore between a rock and a hard place, and the events at Homestead had all the makings of a political disaster no matter what action he took.

Two hours after Sheriff McCleary sent his first telegram to the governor, he sent a second, urging Pattison to "act at once." The governor replied noncommittally by asking how many deputies McCleary had available and what actions he had taken to quell the violence. McCleary again telegraphed the governor at 2:00 p.m., asking for state militia, but Pattison did not respond. Meanwhile, individuals friendly to the strikers communicated with the advisory committee by telegram and advised them that the governor had refused to send state militia, which was not exactly true—Pattison had simply not made a decision one way or the other. Nonetheless, this was interpreted in Homestead as a victory of sorts and may have further emboldened the strikers, who again tried to set fire to the *Iron Mountain* and the *Monongahela* at 2:00 p.m., this time by pumping oil onto the barges and igniting it.

Events had not unfolded the way that Carnegie and Frick had hoped. Although Carnegie and Frick had their uprising, the Pinkertons had failed to retake the works and Magee had thus far been unable to convince the governor to dispatch the state militia. Worse, Sheriff McCleary had held a press conference, which he ended by saying that he had no idea who had called in the Pinkertons; he was clearly trying to save his political future (sheriff was an elected position) by distancing himself from events that were rapidly devolving into a fiasco. At the same time, however, he and Magee worked behind the scenes to try to end the standoff. They spoke with William Weihe late in the afternoon and asked the AAISW president to travel to Homestead and use his influence with the strikers to arrange for the remaining Pinkertons to leave the town unharmed. In exchange, McCleary promised that no more Pinkertons would be sent to Homestead. This was a desperate bargain, representing a concession to one of the strikers' most important demands. Weihe agreed and quickly set off for Homestead.

In the meantime, Governor Pattison was still equivocating, perhaps hoping that the situation would resolve itself. Shortly after his meeting with Weihe, McCleary received a telegram from Pattison, again refusing state militia troops. Later, at a press conference, Pattison praised Homestead's citizens as "industrious, hard-working, intelligent people" and asserted that the "[. . .] civil authorities must in the end settle the differences."[35] While on the surface, the governor's actions seemed to favor the strikers (that was how they were treated in Homestead), Pattison also asserted during his press conference that

> the sheriff must exhaust all of his authority before the state will interfere. The state lends its aid when the local authorities are overborne. The sheriff has but twelve deputies up to the present time, his ordinary force. If the emergency is as great as alleged, *he should have employed a thousand.*[36]

For his part, Pattison was hedging. On one hand, he praised the strikers, while on the other hand, he set a clear bar for state intervention.

Sheriff McCleary moved to meet that bar by subpoenaing 105 of Allegheny County's most prominent men to serve as a sheriff's posse. These men (who were instructed to provide their own weapons and food) were required to assemble at McCleary's office at 9:00 a.m. the following morning before setting out for Homestead. As many of the newspapers noted, the group of people that McCleary had subpoenaed would hardly be an effective fighting force; most were too old and not physically fit enough for the type of arduous combat necessary to put down the vastly larger force of strikers. However, these reports missed the point: McCleary simply had to demonstrate to Governor Pattison that he had exhausted all possible remedies in order to give the governor political cover for dispatching the state militia. The goal was not to actually *do something*, because McCleary had already concluded that that was impossible. Rather, it was to *look* as though he had exhausted all possibilities, thereby forcing Pattison to act.

At roughly the same time that McCleary was subpoenaing his posse, Weihe arrived in Homestead to try to secure safe passage for the Pinkertons out of town. The scene that greeted Weihe must have shocked him: an armed crowd, swelled by thousands of workers from surrounding areas, some trying to flood the river with oil while others stood ready with dynamite, poised to hurl the explosives at the ships. Word quickly spread of Weihe's arrival, and the AAISW president mounted a boiler to address the crowd. He recounted McCleary's offer—to let the Pinkertons go safely and they would not return—but was greeted with hoots and shouts of "no." Weihe's address was even interrupted by a series of explosions caused by fireworks that some of the workers had fired at *Iron Mountain* and the *Monongahela* in an attempt to ignite the ships.

In an attempt to regain control of the crowd, advisory committee member Hugh O'Donnell mounted a pile of steel beams and hoisted an American flag over his head. Addressing the crowd, he said that Weihe's plan made a lot of sense and was worth considering. Workers began shouting out suggestions, including one that the strikers should hold the men until Sheriff McCleary arrived to arrest each of the Pinkertons for murder. This idea provoked an explosion of support, and O'Donnell jumped down from the beams and moved toward the barges to negotiate the Pinkertons' terms of surrender.

At about 6:00 p.m., two Pinkertons emerged from the *Iron Mountain*'s cabin, holding white handkerchiefs. They proceeded to negotiate with O'Donnell and two other advisory committee members. O'Donnell described the surrender terms, in part: he promised them safe passage from Homestead but said nothing about being arrested and tried for murder. More important, O'Donnell personally guaranteed the Pinkertons' safety, a crucial part of getting them to leave the (relative) safety of the ships' cabins. Yet, as O'Donnell escorted the first group of Pinkertons off the ships, the crowd began screaming, "Kill the detectives!"[37] The moment O'Donnell stepped off the gangplank, scores of angry strikers flooded onto the ships. A striker named Thomas Weldon accidentally shot himself in the stomach after trying to break one Pinkerton's rifle. The sight of Weldon's corpse being carried enraged the crowd, who began abusing the Pinkertons as they exited the ships. Strikers jeered the Pinkertons by threatening all manner of violence, and they may have pelted the detectives with sand and rocks (accounts differ). The strikers also formed a "gauntlet" nearly 600 yards long through which the Pinkertons were forced to march. From both sides, the strikers tripped and hit the Pinkertons, all while astonished reporters watched. Men and women used whatever was handy—sticks, clubs, rifle butts—to beat the defeated agents. One woman even knocked a Pinkerton's eye out with the tip of her umbrella. The Pinkertons begged for mercy, but to no avail. The crowd was determined to take revenge for their fallen comrades. The gauntlet seriously injured approximately half the Pinkertons. One of them, James O'Day, was so badly injured that he later threw himself from a train due to the delirium caused by his injuries.[38] Though the newspapers (many of them sympathetic to Carnegie and Frick) later overstated the violence, it is clear that the crowd did some very real physical damage to the Pinkertons, and the agents feared they might be killed by the mob.

One Pinkerton, a student named John Holway, who had joined the agency to make some quick cash, managed to escape before being put through the gauntlet. He was one of the last to leave the barges and saw how the men ahead of him were being abused as they made their way toward the works. Dropping his bag and pulling his hat low, Holway managed to blend in with the crowd and was making his way out to the street when someone screamed, "A Pinkerton! He's getting away!" Holway broke into a run and ducked into a side street, but a small crowd of men soon found him. They beat Holway with stones for a few minutes until some advisory committee members on patrol rescued the would-be escapist. They took him to the Homestead opera house, where the rest of the Pinkertons were being held. Such was the irony of the situation: Holway owed his life to some of the very men who, earlier in the day, had been trying very hard to kill him.

After the majority of Pinkertons had passed through the gauntlet into the works, the strikers descended on the *Iron Mountain* and the *Monongahela*, stripping the ships of useful items before setting them on fire. Once the burning ships disappeared into the river, the crowd assembled the dazed and beaten Pinkertons and marched the hated detectives through Homestead's streets. On the march to the opera house, which the advisory committee had decided would serve as a temporary jail, town residents abused the Pinkertons. One Pinkerton who tried to escape was chased down and savagely beaten by a woman before being dragged into the opera house, and the last detective in line was savagely beaten by a club-wielding member of the crowd. The violence got so intense that some of the guards appointed by the advisory committee actually turned their guns on the crowd to protect the Pinkertons from further abuse. Only the swift intervention of Burgess McLuckie prevented the situation from getting further out of hand.

Shortly after corralling the Pinkertons in Homestead's opera house, the advisory committee met with the borough council to formulate a plan for transferring their prisoners to Sheriff McCleary. Since these two bodies overlapped to a considerable degree, both organizations worked easily together and quickly arrived at the decision that McCleary could take the Pinkertons into his custody provided he did so with only a single deputy and on the condition that he charge all of them with murder. At roughly the same time, AAISW president William Weihe was meeting in Pittsburgh with McCleary, Christopher Magee, the union's attorney, and various members of the union's leadership to discuss how best to handle the situation. Eventually, they decided that McCleary should take the Pinkertons into custody, and at around 1:00 a.m., they all boarded a train headed for Homestead. Once in Homestead, McCleary took custody of the Pinkertons and marched them onto the train for the return trip to Pittsburgh. In addition, 50 strikers joined McCleary and Magee on the train.

When they arrived in Pittsburgh, Sheriff McCleary spoke with the superintendent of Pittsburgh's police force about what to do with the Pinkertons. Reporters on the train described the discussion as "intense," and the train was eventually moved to the Pennsylvania Railroad's yards on Eighteenth Street, where Magee and McCleary announced that the agents were not going to be arrested or charged.[39] The union's lawyer, William J. Brennan, voiced his support of their plan, and the Pinkertons departed Pittsburgh at 10:00 a.m. on a Pennsylvania Railroad train bound for Philadelphia. Two days later, Brennan would urge the strikers to relinquish control of the works to the company, a move that won him no friends in the union; the advisory committee flatly denied his request.

The day was over. As peace settled over Homestead, it was unclear who had won. The Pinkertons had been repulsed, but for how long? Would Carnegie and Frick honor their agreement not to send more? Moreover, even as the guns fell silent, the battle for public opinion—a crucial front in the overall war between Carnegie Steel and its employees at Homestead—was just heating up.

NOTES

1 William Serrin, *Homestead: The Glory and Tragedy of an American Steel Town* (New York, NY: Times Books, 1992), 30–34.
2 Ibid., 20–21.
3 James H. Bridge, *A Romance of Millions: The Inside History of the Carnegie Steel Company* (New York, NY: Aldine, 1903), 150–158.
4 David Nasaw, *Andrew Carnegie* (New York, NY: The Penguin Press, 2006), 213.
5 Ibid., 250.
6 Paul Krause, *The Battle for Homestead, 1880–1892: Politics, Culture, and Steel* (Pittsburgh, PA: University of Pittsburgh Press, 1992), 242–243.
7 Nasaw, *Andrew Carnegie*, 404.
8 Les Standiford, *Meet You in Hell* (New York: Crown, 2005), 142.
9 Ibid., 149.
10 Joseph Frazier Wall, *Andrew Carnegie* (Pittsburgh, PA: University of Pittsburgh Press, 1989), 540.
11 Nasaw, *Andrew Carnegie*, 406–407; and Krause, *The Battle for Homestead, 1880–1892*, 290.

12 Nasaw, *Andrew Carnegie*, 406–407; and Wall, *Andrew Carnegie*, 549–551.

13 Wall, *Andrew Carnegie*, 544–545. Emphasis mine.

14 Krause, *The Battle for Homestead, 1880–1892*, 42.

15 Nasaw, *Andrew Carnegie*, 415.

16 Standiford, *Meet You in Hell*, 141.

17 Ibid., 117.

18 Ibid., 144.

19 Ibid., 132.

20 "Went by Rail, Back by Boat," *Pittsburg Dispatch*, July 6, 1892, in *"The River Ran Red": Homestead 1892*, Ed. David P. Demarest, Jr. (Pittsburgh, PA: University of Pittsburgh Press, 1992), 67.

21 Nasaw, *Andrew Carnegie*, 418–421; Standiford, *Meet You in Hell*, 151; and Wall, *Andrew Carnegie*, 557.

22 "Investigation of the Employment of Pinkerton Detectives in Connection with the Labor Troubles at Homestead, PA" (Washington, DC: Government Printing Office, 1892), 52.

23 Ibid., 105.

24 Krause, *The Battle for Homestead, 1880–1892*, 16–17.

25 Ibid., 18.

26 Ibid.

27 Ibid., 20.

28 Ibid.

29 Ibid.

30 Ibid., 22.

31 Standiford, *Meet You in Hell*, 175.

32 Krause, *The Battle for Homestead, 1880–1892*, 25.

33 Ibid.

34 "Investigation of the Employment of Pinkerton Detectives in Connection with the Labor Troubles at Homestead, PA," 57.

35 Krause, *The Battle for Homestead, 1880–1892*, 32.

36 Ibid. Emphasis mine.

37 Ibid., 33.

38 Serrin, *Homestead*, 81.

39 Krause, *The Battle for Homestead, 1880–1892*, 40.

CHAPTER 5

Aftermath

Two very different narratives of the events at Homestead quickly emerged in the days that followed: one that defended the strikers against Carnegie and Frick's attempt to forcibly take the works and hire replacement workers, and another that celebrated the right of private property and stoked fears of anarchism. For instance, Joseph Pulitzer's *New York World*, one of the Democratic Party's leading newspapers, depicted Frick as smoking while "blood flowed" in Homestead. *The St. Paul Globe*, also a strongly Democratic newspaper, declared, "The dogs of war unleashed and redden their fangs in the heart's blood of locked-out workmen and hired thugs." The paper's editors even called the Pinkertons' attempt to retake the Homestead works a "treacherous attempt at an uncalled-for coup de main responsible for a terrific crime at early dawn." On July 9, 1892, even the generally Republican-leaning *Wichita Daily Eagle* reported that "three of the victims of the Pinkertons' bullets" had been laid to rest, and the union's members were "quietly awaiting the next move of the Carnegie company." Conversely, *The Pittsburg Dispatch* headlined an article about the Pinkertons, "Like Rats in a Trap," and gave an entire column to "Pinkerton men tell of the awful agony they endured on the barges." Later that week, the *New York Times* opined that "mob rule in Homestead has come to an inglorious end," though the paper's editors did question Frick's obstinacy in refusing to negotiate with the AAISW.[1]

Thus, in the days following the violence at Homestead, a new battle—that for public opinion—raged; it was a battle both sides were committed to winning. Uncharacteristically, Frick took the fight for public opinion so seriously that when the postmaster of Munhall, Pennsylvania (a borough in Allegheny County adjoining Homestead), had boasted to a reporter that "we cleared the Pinkertons out," he contacted U.S. Postmaster

General, noted department store millionaire John Wannamaker, and demanded that Wannamaker investigate the matter and discipline the offender.[2] While there is no record this actually happened, it demonstrates the lengths to which Frick was willing to go to punish anyone connected with the strike.

Yet, while Frick and the company were out in the public eye, Carnegie remained strangely silent about the violence. Undoubtedly, this reflected Carnegie's desire not to undercut Frick and his own interest in not being criticized for the violence. At the Dunalastair Hotel in Kinlock Rannoch, Carnegie responded to a question asked by a reporter from the *New York World* by calling the strike "deplorable" and pointing out that the strike had not taken place in the "old" Carnegie works (presumably Edgar Thomson) but in the "recently acquired" Homestead mills.[3] This assertion was typically disingenuous, and Carnegie's goal seems to have been to suggest that longtime company employees would never strike or commit acts of violence. Of course, his statement ignores the fact that he had owned the Homestead works for nine years and had experienced similar labor troubles at his other steel mills.

Perhaps because this line of reasoning was too absurd (even for a serial dissembler such as Carnegie), the industrialist simply began refusing to answer questions about Homestead, saying only that he was retired from business, had no active role in the company's day-to-day management, and had no opinion on the violence. At one point, he stormed out of an interview after the reporter asked questions about Homestead and pressed Carnegie on his answers; as a result, the story (which was picked up by other newspapers in the United States) depicted the industrialist as arrogant, unconcerned with the violence, insulting, and pretentious. Moreover, the reporter took pains to note that Carnegie had spent $10,000 renting a hunting lodge and was attended by a group of uniformed servants, drawing an unfavorable comparison between the millionaire's extravagant spending and his company's claims that it needed to cut wages to remain competitive.

The bad press did not stop at the water's edge: many prominent European newspapers criticized both the company's tactics and Carnegie personally for the events at Homestead. *The Times* in London attacked Carnegie personally for the use of the Pinkertons, calling him a "Scotch-Yankee plutocrat" and contrasting him with the "wretched workman" who made possible Carnegie's summer vacations.[4] The *Glasgow Trades Counsel* sarcastically thanked Carnegie for calling attention to workingmen's struggles and then denounced the industrialist as a "new Judas Iscariot." Various British civic and workingmen's groups voted to refuse any future gifts from Carnegie, and a Member of Parliament to whose campaign Carnegie had donated sent the donation to AAISW to be added to the union's strike fund.[5] As a result, Carnegie told everyone who would listen that he was no longer engaged in the company's day-to-day business and had nothing to do with the events at Homestead, but that was totally untrue.

In reality, Frick kept Carnegie well informed of the developments in Homestead and the reaction to the company's actions in the press. The day after the violence, Carnegie telegraphed Frick and (perhaps out of some fear that the younger man would lose his nerve as Abbott had in 1889) praised his resolve. "All anxiety gone since you stand firm," Carnegie wrote. "Never employ one of these rioters. Let grass grow over the works. Must not fail now. You will easily win next trial."[6] Frick responded with a detailed letter on July 11 in which he recounted the previous days' events, placing the blame for the Pinkertons' failure to land on Potter, who, Frick complained, "[. . .] did not show the nerve I expected he would." The following day, Carnegie wrote to Frick, encouraging the younger man to enlist more Pinkerton agents, but only if they were willing to wait the strikers out. Carnegie also bemoaned Governor Pattison's unwillingness to dispatch the state militia, stating, "No Governor can afford to let a mob conquer."[7]

The distance from the events clouded Carnegie's judgment; even now, he recommended sending more Pinkerton agents to Homestead, deluding himself into thinking that the violence that had broken out a few days earlier would not be repeated if the agents just showed more resolve. Thousands of miles away, Carnegie refused to accept responsibility for the fact that *any* attempt by the company to reassert control over the works was likely to lead to violence, and he also took steps to distance himself from the events at Homestead, telling an Associated Press reporter on June 7 that he had "[. . .] not attended to business for the past three years," but that he had "implicit confidence in those who are managing the mills."[8] The statement implied that he was totally removed from the planning and execution of the events at Homestead when the very opposite was true. Privately, Carnegie confided to his cousin that the events at Homestead had been a "fiasco," but that he (Carnegie) had to keep quiet and support Frick to defeat the union. Carnegie was already engaged in creating the myth that he had little or nothing to do with what had happened at Homestead and that things would have been different if only he had been in charge, lies that he repeated so often throughout the rest of his life that he convinced even himself.

However, on another level, Carnegie's physical distance from the events rocking Homestead did prevent him from fully understanding their meaning. Bemoaning the disappearance of the allegedly "pleasant relations" that had once existed between management and labor at Homestead, Carnegie told Frick that the strikers who did not return to work should simply be replaced, but conversely, the company would "[. . .] give every man a certificate according to his merits, which may enable him to find satisfactory employment. Without anger and with deep regret [. . .] our paths are now separate—we can labor together no more."[9] The lessons of Homestead had not penetrated Carnegie's mind, and he seems to have believed that the battle was nothing more than a regrettable difference of opinion that could be settled with a handshake and a letter of recommendation. In a sense, Carnegie had actually begun believing his own lies.

On July 7, the day after the Pinkertons were repulsed, an eerie calm settled over Homestead. The advisory committee had assigned men to patrol the streets and others to repair any damage to the works caused by the fighting, because it was important to show the world that the strikers respected private property. The Pinkertons had been successfully repulsed but at a devastating cost. Though over the next few days some people composed and sung ballads about the strikers' heroic expulsion of the Pinkertons or hung posters celebrating "The Battle of Fort Frick," the predominate mood was a sober calm born of the recognition that victory was still an uphill battle. The strikers were in a fight to the death and fully expected the company to send an even larger force of Pinkertons to attempt once again to take control of the works.

Meanwhile, back in Pittsburgh, the company was adding fuel to the fire. As McCleary was collecting the defeated Pinkertons, Carnegie Steel's secretary, Francis Lovejoy, issued a statement that condemned the violence, asserted that the strikers should be charged with murder, and gloated that the company would never again deal with the AAISW or any other union. Clearly, the events of the last 48 hours had not given the company's management pause. If anything, Frick and Carnegie remained fully committed to use this episode, which they had practically engineered, as cover for breaking the AAISW.

The strikers' anger had not abated either. If anything, it had grown. It was stoked from the Fourth Avenue Methodist Episcopal Church's pulpit by Reverend John McIlyar, who asserted, "The existence of this union of men was threatened by a body of Pinkertons." Of Frick, McIlyar said angrily:

> This town is bathed in tears today and it is all brought about by one man, who is less respected by the laboring people than any other employer in the country. There is no more sensibility in that man than in a toad.[10]

That same day, the works' superintendent, John A. Potter, appeared in town and demanded access to the buildings but was refused entry by the union's guards. Emboldened by what they perceived as a victory the day before, the strikers were not about to simply give up just because Potter asked them to.

As angry as the strikers were, they were also conscious of not going too far (relatively speaking). That evening, a group of anarchists arrived in town and began distributing leaflets arguing that the workers owned the works and should just seize the buildings. In very short order, two of the anarchists were arrested, and the rest were forced to leave town.[11] On July 10, the advisory committee reformed itself in order to provide necessary leadership, control the rowdier strikers, and speak to the press with a single, unified voice. It was the advisory committee that issued a statement on July 14 cautioning AAISW lodges at other Carnegie mills not to undertake sympathy strikes because it would give Frick an excuse to attack the unions at those mills as well.

Two days after the battle, Sheriff McCleary returned to town, saying that he was now willing to accept the advisory committee's offer of men to be deputized to protect the works. They rebuffed him, and he returned to Pittsburgh by train empty-handed. This was, in part, due to Hugh O'Donnell that same day leading a small group of strikers to Harrisburg, where they conferred with Governor Pattison. The strikers considered Pattison sympathetic to their cause, a perception he reinforced by implying that he would not mobilize the state militia to retake the works. O'Donnell's group returned to Homestead confident that they could hold the works (which were now stocked with weapons and ammunition) indefinitely. The advisory committee perceived McCleary as more interested in protecting Carnegie Steel's interests than in doing what was (from their perspective) right, so they decided to hold the works on their own authority.

Unfortunately for the strikers, the tide was already turning. Governor Pattison, still trying to find a way out of the situation that did not offend his powerful political patrons or the people who had elected him, had dispatched an emissary to the region to get a sense of whether any possibility existed for a negotiated settlement. The emissary, a state militia officer, reported that the strikers were committed to preventing the importation of scab labor and that any attempt by the company to bring in new workers would lead to bloodshed. Conversely, Frick refused to negotiate with or even recognize the AAISW. In other words, both sides had staked their positions and neither would compromise. Pattison had a decision to make: support the strikers or the company. On July 10, Sheriff McCleary telegraphed Governor Pattison, saying:

> I have failed to secure a posse respectable enough in numbers to accomplish anything, and I am satisfied that no posse raised by

civil authority can do anything to change the condition of affairs and that any attempt by an inadequate force to restore the right of law will only result in further armed resistance and consequent loss of life.[12]

McCleary's telegraph finally forced the governor to make a decision. That evening, Pattison decided to dispatch more than 8,000 state militia troops to Homestead; they were en route early the following morning.

Shortly after drafting the militia's orders, Pattison notified McCleary that he had sent the militia and asked the sheriff to get in touch with the commanding general, George R. Snowden, on the latter's arrival. Word of Pattison having called up the militia reached Homestead within an hour of the governor's order, so that by 2:00 p.m. on July 11, the townspeople gathered at the opera house to discuss the development. While the *Boston Evening Telegraph* asserted that some strikers remained defiant and expressed the belief that they could repel the militia, these individuals were clearly in the minority. Many more strikers were confident that Pattison, who they still viewed as sympathetic to their cause, was dispatching the militia

Figure 5.1 The Pennsylvania state militia encampment at Homestead.
Courtesy of Rivers of Steel National Heritage Area.

to *help* them, a view reinforced by Burgess McLuckie, who at one point during the meeting exclaimed, "We don't want the Pinkertons here. We want the militia." The strike leaders lectured the crowd that they had to treat the militiamen respectfully and claimed that the advisory committee would punish *anyone* (women and children included) who failed to do so.[13] McLuckie and O'Donnell even formed a welcoming committee to meet the militia when it arrived, and members of the town's four brass bands were alerted so that they would be present when the troops' trains arrived.

The 8,500 state militiamen did not arrive until close to 9:00 a.m. the following morning. Less than half an hour after they arrived, some troops had entered the works and established sentry posts while others had formed themselves into a line of battle 4,000 men long on the hill overlooking the town. These men, as a consequence of the Pennsylvania state militia's embarrassing performance during the Great Railroad Strike of 1877, were among the best-trained state militiamen in the country. Major General George R. Snowden was a highly experienced Civil War veteran appointed to the position two years earlier. He was a lifelong Pennsylvanian who fought at Antietam, Fredericksburg, Chancellorsville, and Gettysburg. When O'Donnell and a group of local notables went to meet the general, it did not go well. After O'Donnell informed Snowden that he represented both the citizens of Homestead and the strikers, the general ambiguously replied that he was always glad to meet good citizens of any community. When O'Donnell asserted that he and the people he represented had been peaceful, law-abiding citizens, Snowden tersely replied, "No, you have not. You have not been peaceful and law-abiding." Perhaps trying to impress the general, O'Donnell responded that the town had four brass bands standing at the ready to celebrate the militia's appearance. Snowden dismissed the bands, saying first, "I don't want any brass band business while I'm here," and then telling O'Donnell, "I want you to distinctly understand that I am master of this situation."[14] It had suddenly become clear: the state militia had come not as allies, but as occupiers.

The state of Pennsylvania spent $22,000 per day maintaining the militiamen in Homestead, an astonishing sum in an era when most of the laborers at Carnegie's steel mills made a few hundred dollars per year.

Implicit in the militia's mandate to protect the company's property and prevent violence was the understanding that Snowden would break the strike. No other resolution was possible. The militia would take control of the works and turn them over to Carnegie and Frick, who would immediately move to import scabs or force the strikers to sign individual contracts. Less than a week after the militia arrived, the company had imported 100 new workers, housing them in the works to limit the scabs' exposure to townspeople. The company moved quickly to exploit the militia's presence. On July 15, the company relit some of the furnaces, sending smoke billowing through the works' massive chimneys. As a result, a group of strikers tried to storm the works and were only turned back when the militiamen leveled their rifles, bayonets fixed, at the men. The next day, leaflets appeared all over town announcing the company's policy of hiring back any worker who had not taken part in the "disturbances" earlier in the month; this was countered on July 22 by another leaflet arguing that the workers' labor and the tariff that made Carnegie's empire so profitable had "earned" the public an ownership stake in the works. The arrival of another tugboat carrying replacement workers was the company's only reply to this argument.[15]

To make matters worse, the militia acted in ways that seemed calculated to offend the strikers. For instance, Snowden hired the *Little Bill*, the tugboat that had pulled the Pinkertons' ships into Homestead, to transport supplies. At least some of these supplies were used to construct houses within the works' gates, and the company let it be known that these new residences would be for the new laborers that it had hired to replace the strikers. As a result, public affection for the militia quickly dropped; the *Pittsburgh Press* noted, "[. . .] the apparent indifference shown on the part of the ladies of Homestead for the soldiers [. . .] There have been very few visitors of the gentler sex at Camp Black."[16]

The ongoing newspaper coverage of the strike and its aftermath (much of it inflammatory and partisan) prompted both the House of Representatives and the Senate to investigate events at Homestead. As noted previously, 1892 was an election year, and members of Congress sensed an opportunity for some free publicity. The House Judiciary Committee was already investigating the Pinkerton Agency's practices in breaking a series of railroad strikes, so the investigation into the events at Homestead was merely an expansion of those hearings. Headed by Representative William C. Oates, a Democrat from Alabama (and former Confederate general), the proceedings lasted for three days and were as much about embarrassing Republicans in an election year and discrediting the tariff as they were about getting to the bottom of what had happened at Homestead. Frick was grilled extensively about the wages he paid his workers, about conditions in the mill, and why the tariff had not produced the benefits for laborers that its supporters claimed it would. For his part, Frick refused to answer questions about the company's operating costs and responded to questions about the tariff by arrogantly noting that he had never asked Congress to pass it. At one point, he boldly asserted, "We have never given a thought to what effect our affairs might have on either of the political parties," a statement that must have left a few Republicans anxious about the outcome of the November presidential election shaking their heads in disgust.[17]

Time was not on the strikers' side. Though the AAISW reported it had sufficient money on hand to support its members during a protracted strike, only a small minority of Homestead workers were union members; the rest, whose refusal to work had been a crucial step in bringing production to a halt, had nothing on which they could fall back. Frick knew time was on his side, but he was not above gloating. On July 19, the company's secretary, Francis Lovejoy, called the strikers "sheep," asserting that once a few came back to work, the rest would follow.[18]

The worst was yet to come. While McCleary had reneged on his promise to charge the Pinkertons with murder, warrants were drawn up for the arrest of McLuckie, O'Donnell, and six other strikers; they were charged with murder in the death of Thomas Connors, the Pinkerton guard who had bled to death from an arm wound during the battle. Three constables, protected by two companies of militiamen, combed the streets of Homestead, looking for the men. The hostile townspeople refused to assist in the search, but the men, who had been alerted about their impending arrest, had fled the town.

The following month, O'Donnell and another group of strikers were arrested and charged with the murder of Pinkerton J. W. Klein. A few weeks later, many more strikers were arrested on various charges that ranged from riot, to conspiracy, to murder. Eventually, 167 strikers were charged with felonies related to the events at Homestead. Shockingly, on September 30, the Pennsylvania Supreme Court had issued warrants against the AAISW's entire advisory committee on the charge of treason. With the flurry of prosecutions, McCleary had to swear in a special group of deputies specifically assigned to apprehending and arresting strikers charged with crimes related to Homestead.[19] The strikers, who had felt so confident just a few weeks earlier, now faced long prison sentences in Western State Penitentiary if convicted.

The union fought back by also availing itself of the legal system, but it was at a grave disadvantage. In early August, Hugh Ross, a prominent striker and one of the men charged with murder, swore out arrest warrants for Henry Clay Frick, Carnegie Steel executive John G. A. Leishman, company secretary Francis Lovejoy, mill superintendent John Potter, Pinkerton captain Frederick Heinde, and William and Robert Pinkerton (owners of the Pinkerton Agency), among others. Pittsburgh Alderman Festus M. King duly issued the warrants, and the men eventually appeared before Judge Nathaniel Ewing, who released Frick on a $10,000 bond and later observed that he did not believe the murder charges against the defendants could be sustained because, in his opinion, the strikers had illegally occupied the works and the Pinkertons were on company property at the invitation of Carnegie Steel's chairman. Given Ewing's background as a Republican and former counsel for both the Pennsylvania Railroad and H. C. Frick & Company, his conclusion in the case should come as no surprise. For the strikers, however, using the court system (administered by political appointees dependent upon the city's political bosses) made them David to Carnegie Steel's Goliath.

No one could have predicted what happened next. On July 23, an anarchist named Alexander Berkman tried to assassinate Frick.

The strikers had worked hard to distance themselves from the anarchist movement to gain public support and sympathy. Berkman's actions, which

Anarchism

Anarchism is a political philosophy that argues that states (organized communities governed by a unified government) are harmful to individual liberty and therefore advocates stateless societies. While there are many different strands of anarchism, all adherents are referred to as anarchists. Fear of anarchism was particularly pronounced in the United States during the late nineteenth and early twentieth centuries.

The word "anarchy" is defined from the Greek word *anarchos*, which means "without rulers." The word "anarchy" was first used in 1539, though precedents for anarchism can be found in political writings that appeared at least as early as the sixth century BC. By the 1790s, Maximilien de Robespierre was using the term "anarchists" to attack his political opponents. The first political philosopher to describe himself as an "anarchist" was Pierre-Joseph Proudhon (1809–1865), a member of France's Parliament whose writings in the 1840s laid out much of anarchism's main tenets. Beginning in the early 1880s, some anarchists began advocating "propaganda of the deed," by which they meant an action designed to be an example to witnesses. Usually, these deeds included terroristic actions such as bombings or assassinations. Beginning in the 1880s, anarchists tried to assassinate Germany's Kaiser Wilhelm I, Italy's King Umberto I, and Russia's Tsar Alexander II. In 1901, Leon Czlolgosz (who later claimed to be influenced by prominent American anarchists such as Emma Goldman) succeeded in killing President William McKinley. Propaganda of the deed fell out of favor among anarchists following the outbreak of World War I in 1914, though some intermittent acts of terrorism (such as the 1920 Wall Street bombing) continued well into the twentieth century.

had no connection to the strikers or the advisory committee, were nonetheless perceived (due to largely slanted media coverage) as proof that labor unionism was the same thing as anarchism and a threat to the country. Berkman was born in 1870 in Vilnius, the capital of Lithuania (a part of the Russian Empire at the time). His family later relocated to St. Petersburg, where he spent much of his childhood. In 1888, he immigrated to New York City, where he became heavily involved with the anarchist movement. Falling under the sway of Johann "Johnny" Most, a prominent anarchist who promoted the concept of "propaganda of the deed" (political actions meant to provide an example to other revolutionaries), Berkman advocated the release of the men convicted of the 1886 Haymarket Riot. It was during this time that he met Emma Goldman, a young anarchist and free-love advocate.

Angered by Carnegie Steel's attempts to break the AAISW and Frick's high-handed refusal to negotiate with the union, Berkman and Goldman plotted to assassinate the industrialist. Their plan involved a comedy of errors—initially, Berkman was going to kill Frick with a bomb, but the anarchist proved inept at bomb-making—and some embarrassing setbacks —Goldman tried to finance the operation through prostitution, but her only client gave her money out of pity and sent her home—but eventually they decided that Berkman would travel to Pittsburgh, ambush Frick, and shoot the industrialist to death. Goldman's role (aside from her abortive attempt to finance the operation) was to explain Berkman's motives to the newspapers after his death.

In late July, Berkman purchased a suit with some borrowed money and traveled to Pittsburgh via train. The anarchist followed Frick from the Duquesne Club, where the industrialist had eaten his lunch, to the company's office. Berkman, claiming that his name was Simon Bachman and that he represented an employment agency that could supply the company with laborers to replace those who had struck in Homestead, had repeatedly tried to see Frick, but he had been unsuccessful. The anarchist had shown up that morning, but Frick's secretary said that the industrialist was busy and asked Berkman to return later that afternoon.

While Frick was meeting with another Carnegie Steel executive, John G. A. Leishman, Berkman forced his way into his office and brandished a revolver. As Frick jumped to his feet, Berkman fired. The bullet hit the industrialist's earlobe before entering his neck. As Frick lay on the ground, Berkman fired a second time, again striking his victim's neck. Momentarily stunned, Leishman jumped from his chair and grabbed Berkman, whose third shot went wild. The bullet embedded itself in the wall close to the ceiling. As Leishman and the anarchist struggled, Frick staggered to his feet to help subdue Berkman. Frick and Leishman wrestled Berkman to the floor,

Emma Goldman (1869–1940)

Emma Goldman was a prominent anarchist, feminist, and free-love advocate. Born in present-day Lithuania to an orthodox Jewish family, Goldman's childhood and adolescence was mostly unhappy. Partially as a result, she immigrated to the United States in 1885, eventually settling in New York City. During her first day in New York, she was introduced to Alexander Berkman, a young anarchist who invited Emma to accompany him to a lecture that evening. It was this lecture that first introduced Goldman to Johann Most, one of the most vocal proponents of both anarchism and "propaganda of the deed."

Embracing anarchism following the Haymarket Riot in 1886, Goldman became a prominent writer and lecturer, eventually founding the radical journal *Mother Earth*. It was she who provided much of the economic support for Berkman's failed attempt to assassinate Frick following the Homestead Strike, and she was later detained in connection with Leon Czolgosz's assassination of President William McKinley in 1901. Her refusal to condemn Czolgosz's actions led to her vilification in the press, and she responded by adopting a new identity and supporting herself by working as a private nurse, though she was eventually drawn back into the public spotlight when Congress passed the Anarchist Exclusion Act in 1903. During World War I, she was arrested for opposing the Selective Service Act of 1917 and was convicted of espionage. After serving two years in prison, she was deported to the Soviet Union in late 1919. Over the next 20 years, she lived in a variety of countries, eventually dying in Toronto, Canada in February 1940. The U.S. Immigration and Naturalization Service allowed her body to enter the United States, and she is buried in a suburb of Chicago, Illinois.

but the anarchist managed to pull out his dagger. Berkman stabbed Frick in the hip, the side, and the leg, but the industrialist held the anarchist tightly. Frick's clerks, alarmed by the gunshots and the sound of struggling, burst through the door and helped their boss subdue Berkman, who was shortly thereafter taken into custody by a sheriff's deputy.

When the deputy had leveled his revolver at Berkman, Frick allegedly cried out, "Don't shoot. Leave him to the law, but raise his head and let me see his face."[20] When the deputy yanked Berkman's head up, Frick pointed out that the anarchist was chewing something. They forced Berkman's mouth open and found a small but powerful explosive made of mercury fulminate. Anarchists had used similar explosives before with deadly efficiency, and just the small capsule in Berkman's mouth would have, if broken, killed everyone in the office. The event was so frightening that, after Berkman was subdued, Leishman feinted.

Berkman was arrested, and Frick was helped to a chaise lounge while one of his clerks summoned medical help. While he and his men waited, Frick had collapsed shortly after Berkman was removed from the office. He then endured two excruciating hours of probing the wounds for the bullets. Once the bullets were removed and the wounds dressed, Frick (who had refused any form of anesthetic) returned to work. Later in the day, he even sent his mother a telegraph that read, "Was shot twice but not dangerously." He then sent Carnegie a telegraph informing the older man of the day's events and ending with a reiteration of the company's stance:

> This incident will not change the attitude of the Carnegie Steel Company toward the Amalgamated Association. I do not think I shall die, but whether I do or not, *the Company will pursue the same policy and it will win.*[21]

Frick's stance was as much a public relations effort as anything else. The company carefully worked to manipulate public sentiment and exact the maximum advantage from the day's events, and it succeeded. While Berkman's attempt to assassinate Frick failed to change the company's attitude toward the AAISW, it decisively moved the general public's sympathies, ironically achieving the opposite of what Berkman had intended.

The story of Frick's near-assassination effectively ended the battle for public opinion in favor of the company. However sympathetic they might have felt toward the workers' grievances, many Americans were genuinely concerned over the purported rise in anarchism in the United States even though the union (which had prided itself on its conservatism) had worked hard to distance itself from more radical elements. Upon meeting some of the Homestead strikers in jail, Berkman was shocked that the union members wanted nothing to do with him; while they expressed unhappiness that Frick was still alive, they did not wish to be associated with anarchism or anarchists such as him. Nevertheless, the press connected the events at Homestead to create the impression that the strikers had been infiltrated (if not outright controlled) by anarchists, and even those newspapers that had supported the strikers editorialized against Berkman's actions. Even the staunchly pro-labor *National Labor Tribune* attacked Berkman, saying, "Whatever the term of imprisonment may be, it will be inadequate to fit this crime—a crime against both capital and the workman."[22] As historian Les Standiford points out, "While the use of Pinkertons to quash a strike had become something of a negative to most Americans, the appearance of bomb-throwing, pistol-blazing radicals as representatives of labor was even more damning."[23]

The pendulum had swung decisively against the strikers, and a pervasive fear of anarchism led to overreaction. For instance, when William Iams, a private in the Pennsylvania militia, exclaimed, "Hooray for the anarchist," in response to reports that Frick had been shot, his commanding officer had him hung by his thumbs. Iams passed out after 20 minutes and was cut down. After he came to, half of Iams' head was shaved (as was custom for disgraced officers), and he was discharged from the state militia. The public was justifiably outraged by the militia's treatment of Iams (the private later unsuccessfully sued his former superiors over the incident), which blunted somewhat the public outcry over Frick's shooting. Nonetheless, the battle for public opinion was more or less over.

In a last-ditch attempt to salvage the strike, Hugh O'Donnell reached out to an unlikely ally: Whitelaw Reid, editor/publisher of the *New-York Tribune* and the Republican Party's nominee for vice president in 1892. As Republicans had feared, the violence at Homestead quickly became a national issue because the Democrats connected it to one of the election's top issues: the tariff on steel. On the same day that the *St. Paul Globe* ran the headline about the "dogs of war" having been unleashed, it ran a political cartoon that explicitly connected William McKinley (future president and author of the tariff bill) to the violence at Homestead. Many prominent Democrats were pointing to the strike as proof that the tariff did not protect American workers the way Republicans had said it would, and the issue refused to go away. Burgess John McLuckie reminded a crowd of strikers in Homestead that they had voted Republican in the hopes that the tariff would ensure higher wages by preventing low-cost imports. Instead of high wages, McLuckie claimed, workers got "[. . .] high fences, Pinkerton detectives, thugs, and militia."[24] Talk such as that, in addition to political cartoons in large-circulation newspapers that implied Republican policies were responsible for the events at Homestead, could shift enough votes to deny Benjamin Harrison a second term as president and Reid a term as vice president. Reid therefore wanted to see the strike ended as quickly as possible.

When O'Donnell contacted Reid, the editor was inclined to listen. The union man told Reid that the strikers were now willing to accept all of the company's terms (the reduction in sliding scale, a contract that expired in winter, etc.) if the company would agree to continue dealing with the union as opposed to signing individual contracts with the workers. This was more or less total capitulation on the union's part, though O'Donnell had not briefed the advisory committee of his plan and had contacted Reid on his own. O'Donnell's plan was simple: could Reid, as a prominent Republican and newspaperman, get in touch with Carnegie and broker the deal? Unfortunately, O'Donnell seems to have bought into

Carnegie's deceptive public statements that he had nothing to do with the day-to-day management of the company and therefore believed (whether it was out of ignorance or desperation is unclear) that Carnegie would be more reasonable than Frick.

Reid was delighted to try to end the strike, and he suggested that O'Donnell write a letter outlining the union's position. Reid would then send the letter to Carnegie. O'Donnell obliged Reid's request, writing, "The spirit that dominates [the strikers] is conciliatory in the extreme, for they deplore the recent sad occurrence as much as any other class of people in the whole country."[25] Reid used his connections to transmit the offer through the office of the American consul in London. Carnegie received the message on July 28 and dithered. On one hand, accepting the terms would bring him the public acclaim he craved and would allow him to foist all the blame for the violence onto Frick. On the other hand, such a move would leave the union intact and permanently damage his relationship with Frick. Deciding that discretion was the better part of valor, Carnegie cabled Frick and explained the situation, leaving Frick to make the final decision. Carnegie then replied to Reid's telegram by saying that the matter was out of his hands and that the editor would need to contact Frick, though he surely knew how the "prince of coke" would react.

Upon receiving Carnegie's telegram, Reid turned up the heat on Frick by sending John Milholland, a prominent member of the Republican National Committee, to plead with the industrialist to accept the deal. Frick, still recovering from the assassination attempt, became quite agitated by the request, telling Milholland that he would not negotiate with the AAISW even if asked by President Harrison himself. Frick's anger was stoked the following week when he received word that Secretary of War Stephen Elkins and U.S. Postmaster General John Wanamaker wanted to meet with him; naturally, Frick assumed they wanted to discuss the strike (in reality, they were trying to solicit a campaign contribution), so he refused and cabled Carnegie to insist that the Scot contact Reid to tell him that the company would not negotiate.

Carnegie eventually did as Frick demanded, but the younger man was furious at what he (correctly) perceived as Carnegie's attempt to interfere with the situation.[26] Moreover, Frick suspected (again, correctly) that Carnegie's actions were motivated, in part, by the older man's desire to blunt criticism of the way the company had handled the strike, exacerbating the tension that had plagued their relationship for years.

Wanamaker rose to fame due to his department store, which is a Philadelphia landmark.

President Harrison lost his bid for re-election to the pro-business Democrat Grover Cleveland, who had served as president from 1885 to 1889. Though historians have debated the actual effect of the

> Homestead, which had heretofore voted reliably Republican, went Democratic in 1892 by a wide margin.

events at Homestead on the election, many prominent members of the Republican Party felt that Frick and Carnegie's response to the strike tilted the election toward the Democrats. Reid was particularly bitter that Frick and Carnegie had spurned his attempts to broker a deal between the strikers and the company. As a result, his newspaper, the *New-York Tribune*, missed few opportunities to criticize the two men, who Reid believed had deprived him of the vice presidency.

In early October, a grand jury returned indictments not only against the strikers, but also against Frick and other company personnel. Two days later, on October 13, the last members of the Pennsylvania state militia were withdrawn from Homestead. Four days later, the strike was fractured when four strikers entered the works and applied for their old jobs; time was clearly on the company's side, and on October 31 Carnegie expressed to Frick his surprise that the workers had been able to sustain the strike for this long.[27] AFL president Samuel Gompers tried to prevent any further defections by coming to Homestead and making vague promises of a nationwide boycott of Carnegie Steel products, but as the weather turned cold and winter approached, more workers began returning to their jobs at the Homestead works, vindicating (at least in Carnegie's mind) the tactic of waiting the men out.[28] The defections gradually eroded morale, and on November 17, 2,000 members of the AAISW petitioned the union's leadership to end the strike. AAISW president William Weihe opposed ending the strike, and a motion to do so was defeated 224 to 129. However, that same day, seeing the writing on the wall, the AAISW's leadership council announced to the strikers they were now free to return to work, which essentially meant the strike was over. At least, this was how Frick interpreted the announcement. The following day, he sent Carnegie a telegram with only a single word: "Victory!" Three days later, he sent a longer telegram, and over the next few days, the two gloated via telegraph over the strike's outcome.

NOTES

1 Les Standiford, *Meet You in Hell* (New York, NY: Crown, 2005), 200.
2 Ibid., 206.
3 David Nasaw, *Andrew Carnegie* (New York, NY: The Penguin Press, 2006), 428.

4   Standiford, *Meet You In Hell*, 221.

5   Joseph Frazier Wall, *Andrew Carnegie* (Pittsburgh, PA: University of Pittsburgh Press, 1989), 573.

6   William Serrin, *Homestead: The Glory and Tragedy of an American Steel Town* (New York, NY: Times Books, 1992), 82.

7   Nasaw, *Andrew Carnegie*, 431.

8   Quoted in James H. Bridge, *A Romance of Millions: The Inside History of the Carnegie Steel Company* (New York, NY: Aldine, 1903), 233.

9   Nasaw, *Andrew Carnegie*, 432.

10   Serrin, *Homestead*, 82.

11   Ibid.

12   "The Militia Called Out, State Troops Will Take Possession of Carnegie's Works," *Boston Evening Transcript*, July 11, 1892, 3.

13   Standiford, *Meet You in Hell*, 192.

14   Serrin, *Homestead*, 85.

15   Ibid., 86.

16   "And the National Guard Uniforms Don't Attract Homestead Maids," *Pittsburg Press*, July 16, 1892, in *"The River Ran Red": Homestead 1892*, Ed. David P. Demarest, Jr. (Pittsburgh, PA: University of Pittsburgh Press, 1992), 148.

17   "Investigation of the Employment of Pinkerton Detectives in Connection with the Labor Troubles at Homestead, PA" (Washington, DC: Government Printing Office, 1892), 33.

18   Standiford, *Meet You in Hell*, 205.

19   Ibid., 199.

20   Serrin, *Homestead*, 87.

21   Ibid., 88. Emphasis mine.

22   "As to Anarchy," *National Labor Tribune* July 30, 1892, in *"The River Ran Red": Homestead 1892*, Ed. David P. Demarest, Jr. (Pittsburgh, PA: University of Pittsburgh Press, 1992), 177.

23   Standiford, *Meet You in Hell*, 212.

24   Arthur Burgoyne, *The Homestead Strike of 1892* (Pittsburgh, PA: University of Pittsburgh Press, 1979), 24–25. Quoted in Nasaw, *Andrew Carnegie*, 438.

25   Nasaw, *Andrew Carnegie*, 564.

26   Ibid., 440–441.

27   Standiford, *Meet You In Hell*, 225.

28   Serrin, *Homestead*, 90.

CHAPTER 6

Legacy and Conclusion

On one level, the costs of the events at Homestead are easy to quantify. According to historian Les Standiford, the strike cost Carnegie Steel approximately $300,000, or roughly 10 percent of its net profits in 1892. The AAISW estimated that the lockout and strike cost Homestead's workers more than four times that amount in wages, and Pennsylvania's taxpayers spent half a million dollars restoring control of the works to the company and protecting the scab workers.[1] On another level, however, these numbers represent only the tip of the iceberg. One reason for the astronomical increases in the company's profits was the decline in wages that was now possible. By removing the right to collectively bargain and destroying the union, the company had effectively destroyed the workers' leverage when it came to protesting wage reductions; Homestead's skilled workers' wages dropped by more than 50 percent as a result. Profits, which jumped 1,000 percent between 1893 and 1899, far outstripped wages in general, the total cost of which increased by less than 50 percent. Charles Schwab, who had succeeded John Potter as Homestead's superintendent, relentlessly cut costs by extracting as much labor as possible from his workers and by replacing men with machines wherever possible. The result was that many men were making less in 1900 than in 1892, and there were always more men than jobs available.[2] In the words of historian David P. Demarest Jr., "For the next half century, every aspect of life in Homestead was dominated by the company and its interests."[3]

The effect of these developments on Homestead was toxic. Hamlin Garland, who visited the town for *McClure's Magazine* in 1894, described the city as "dingy," "squalid and unlovely."

According to Garland, Homestead's inhabitants were "lean men, pale and grimy [. . .] [who] wore a look of stoical indifference [. . .] [and] mainly of the discouraged and sullen type to be found elsewhere where labor

> In addition to being a well-known and respected writer, Hamlin Garland was a dedicated paranormal researcher.

passes into the brutalizing stage of severity."[4] From the company's perspective, the mixture of former strikers and the scabs that had replaced them created a fragmented workforce and led to violence and harassment for years to come. Even the strikers, who had been so united in the effort to repel the Pinkertons, became fractured; Garland interviewed one low-paid worker who complained, "The tonnage men brought it on; they could afford to strike, but we couldn't [. . .] we can't hurt Carnegie by six months' starving. It's *our* ribs that'll show through our shirts."[5] Tensions ran so high that a rash of illnesses at the Homestead works led to accusations that some of the former strikers had poisoned the replacement workers' food! As a result, the company hired spies to ferret out potential labor organizers or other "troublemakers," firing offenders and turning them over to local law enforcement.[6] These actions engendered a great deal of suspicion and fragmentation and ensured that Homestead's wounds never completely healed.

After swift trials, Hugh O'Donnell and the other two strikers charged with murder were acquitted. The charges of treason were dropped shortly

Figure 6.1 Hugh O'Donnell.
Courtesy of Rivers of Steel National Heritage Area.

thereafter. There seemed a movement afoot to put the violence behind everyone, and none of the Carnegie Steel or Pinkerton employees charged with murder over the events at Homestead were ever tried. However, the sentiment to get beyond Homestead had its limits: ever vindictive and petty, Frick and Carnegie blacklisted the strike's leaders, who found themselves unable to secure employment in the iron and steel industry ever again.

McLuckie eventually lost his home, and his wife subsequently became sick and died. Later in life, Carnegie liked to claim that a friend of his had come across McLuckie eking out an existence in the mines of Northern Mexico. The story goes that Carnegie used his influence to secretly secure McLuckie a job on the Sonora Railway, which eventually made the former striker a wealthy man. Told by a mutual acquaintance of Carnegie's secret role in getting him this job, McLuckie is supposed to have exclaimed, "That was damn white of Andy."[7] Many contemporary historians question this story, as there is little evidence to support it and it is exactly the type of self-aggrandizing "tall tale" that Carnegie told throughout his life. Alternatively, Carnegie may have misinterpreted the tone of McLuckie's comment, which the former striker may have meant as a criticism of his former employer. Hugh O'Donnell was even less lucky: in addition to

Figure 6.2 John McLuckie.
Courtesy of Rivers of Steel National Heritage Area.

being blacklisted by the company, he was also ostracized by his fellow strikers. Many viewed him as a sellout for the concessions he had offered Whitelaw Reid. In a letter to political scientist Edward W. Bemis, O'Donnell bemoaned his status, arguing that he had been "shunned" by both the strikers and the company.[8] For both O'Donnell and McLuckie, the strike essentially destroyed their lives.

The events at Homestead, which the AAISW had anticipated as a moment to consolidate its power, proved to be the union's downfall, inaugurating a period of rapid decline. Weakened by its capitulation to Carnegie and Frick, the union was powerless to prevent other companies from de-unionizing their mills as contracts with local lodges expired. When the AAISW tried to revitalize itself through an organizing drive in 1896, the company mercilessly squashed the effort. Three years later, Frick ordered the Homestead works closed when some of the employees created an AAISW lodge; the would-be union organizers' effort failed, and the leaders were blacklisted from the steel industry. Interestingly, Gompers refused AFL support to both efforts. Two of Carnegie's most important competitors, Jones & Laughlin Steel and Illinois Steel, pushed the union aside during the 1890s, and efforts to unionize workers at plants in 1901 were mercilessly crushed. Now called the Amalgamated Association of Iron, Steel, and Tin Workers (when the company had absorbed the American Tin Plate Company, the union allowed those workers to join and changed the organization's name), the union was a shadow of its former self, representing just over half the workers it had in 1892, and that mostly due to the influx of tin workers. Historian Leon Wolff called the Amalgamated in this period a "paper tiger" from which its leaders hoped "a new organism with teeth and claws might emerge."[9] Their hopes were in vain; on June 1, 1909, U.S. Steel (the name adopted by the Carnegie Steel Company after it was sold to J. P. Morgan in 1901) announced that, henceforth, it would be an "open" company, meaning that it would no longer bother negotiating with *any* unions. Though the Amalgamated periodically tried to reassert itself, it found itself unable to reclaim its former power. The organization hit rock bottom in 1919, when an organizing drive resulted in a strike that was crushed when employers imported black and Hispanic scabs. Worse, the AFL gave the strike only tepid support and the public (riled by fears of communism caused by the Russian Revolution) supported the employers. Within a few weeks, Amalgamated strikers began crossing the picket lines and, by 1920, labor unionism in American steel plants was dead.

In at least two ways, however, the strike worked toward labor's favor. Both the Senate and the House committees dispatched parties to investigate the events at Homestead and issued reports that were generally sympathetic to the strikers and critical of both the company's management and the Pinkertons. In addition, the year after the strike, the Pennsylvania General Assembly passed the Kearns Act, a law banning the employment of private police forces; by the turn of the century, 25 other states had passed similar laws. In response to testimony collected at Homestead that employers routinely hired Pinkertons to provoke violent confrontations so that local or state governments would be forced to send militia units, the House of Representatives even passed a law forbidding employers from using private police forces in the District of Columbia; the law identified the Pinkertons by name, a symbol of the aversion to paid strikebreakers that swept across the nation in the months and years following Homestead.

Moreover, while steel unionism lay moribund for more than a decade, like a phoenix it rose from the ashes during the Great Depression. In June 1933, Congress passed and President Franklin Roosevelt signed the National Industrial Recovery Act (NIRA). Though declared unconstitutional two years later, the NIRA resuscitated steel industry unionism by recognizing employees' rights to collectively bargain. Because the AAISW still existed, it had the right to organize the steel, iron, and tin industries. In reality, the union (which had only 5,000 members in 1935) was too weak to effectively capitalize on federal protection of collective bargaining rights, so in October of that year, the delegates to the AFL's annual convention debated whether to step in and organize these industries. After a nine-hour debate, the AFL's delegates voted against organizing America's steel industry, so the following day, John L. Lewis (president of the United Mine Workers of America) organized the Congress of Industrial Organizations (CIO) to help industrial workers exercise the collective bargaining rights recognized under NIRA.

Initially, the CIO tried to work through the AAISW but when relations between the two organizations deteriorated, the CIO relied on the newly formed Steel Workers Organizing Committee to re-unionize America's steel industry. Their efforts paid off and, in 1942, a new union—the United Steelworkers (USW)—was formed. Still in existence, the organization represents nearly 900,000 workers in a variety of industrial occupations. Thus, while the strikers at Homestead lost the battle in 1892, an argument could be made that, more than a century later, they won the war.

By contrast, while Carnegie and Frick undoubtedly won the battle for Homestead, the years that followed were plagued by acrimony, suspicion, and hostility. The year after the strike, Carnegie Steel was embroiled in a scandal over the quality of the armor plates produced at the Homestead works, in part due to the lingering bitterness over the strike. In September 1893, four unidentified Carnegie Steel employees contacted a local lawyer, claiming that some of the company's armor plates did not meet standards

John L. Lewis (1880–1969)

John Llewellyn Lewis was one of the leading figures in organized labor in America during the twentieth century. He served for 40 years (1920–1960) as president of the United Mine Workers of America (UMWA) and was instrumental in the founding of the Congress of Industrial Organizations (CIO), the organization that in turn established the United States Steel Workers of America.

Lewis' career spanned the "golden age" of American unionism, a period he helped inaugurate by successfully organizing the country's industrial workers under the terms of the National Industrial Recovery Act. He was a Roosevelt supporter during the Depression but broke with the president during the 1940 election because he was concerned (accurately) that FDR would take the United States into World War II. In the late 1940s, Lewis was further estranged from the Democratic Party when President Harry Truman denounced postwar UMWA strikes as threats to national security. During the 1950s, the UMWA (under Lewis' leadership) scored some impressive victories, including the Federal Mine Safety Act of 1952. However, Lewis' autocratic style and the general decline of the coal industry weakened the union. Due to the UMWA's decline and a series of legal reforms that weakened his control over the union, Lewis retired in 1960. Four years later, President Lyndon Johnson awarded Lewis the Presidential Medal of Freedom.

described in the company's contract with the Navy. Worse, these employees claimed that some of the company's test results on the plates had been falsified to hide the plates' shortcomings. The lawyer first approached Frick and offered to sell the chairman this information; when Frick rebuffed him, the lawyer approached Secretary of the Navy Hilary Herbert, who offered him 25 percent of any fines imposed on Carnegie Steel. Herbert then convened a secret Navy panel that concluded (after a perfunctory investigation) that the charges were true and fined the company 15 percent of the contract's value.

Carnegie and Frick were aghast and immediately wrote to President Cleveland in an attempt to get the Navy to conduct a new investigation. Cleveland demurred, offering only to reduce the fine to 10 percent of the contract's value. Eventually, the House Committee on Naval Affairs got involved, producing a massive report that essentially concluded that the company had manufactured defective plates and had manipulated internal tests to

Grover Cleveland is the only American president to have served two nonconsecutive terms. Between 1928 and 1934, he was featured on the $1,000 bill.

hide that fact. The committee ultimately imposed the same fine that Cleveland had offered (10 percent of the contract's total), which was built into the price paid for the plates when the government offered the company a five-year renewal of the contract. Never willing to take the blame himself, Carnegie instead blamed "the ghost of Homestead" for the company's problems with the federal government, while Frick blamed Schwab for the quality issues at Homestead.[10] Certainly, many prominent Republicans (who might otherwise have acted to protect the company's interests) were glad to see Carnegie punished because they blamed him for Cleveland's win the previous November.

The strike and its tragic aftermath had taken its toll on Frick as well. In the months following the violence at Homestead, Frick's beard went from brown to snow white. Moreover, it stoked the long-simmering animosity between Frick and Carnegie, which soon burst forth into a great fire. About a year after the strike ended, Carnegie secretly met with one of Frick's chief competitors in the coke business, William J. Rainey. Carnegie was trying to secure additional supplies of coke for the company and possibly diminish Frick's position at Carnegie Steel. Understandably, Frick was incensed and consequently tendered his resignation in mid December 1894. Carnegie dismissed Frick's resignation but, at the same time, denigrated him in letters to their mutual acquaintances. In addition, Carnegie inflamed the situation by attempting to sell a large block of bonds he had received from Frick's coke company as part of their original partnership agreement. To Frick, it seemed that Carnegie was moving to sever the steel company's relationship with H. C. Frick & Company. Frick fired off an angry letter to Carnegie in which he harshly accused the Scot of impugning Frick's reputation and performance. In his response to the letter, Carnegie accepted Frick's resignation. Two weeks later, Carnegie Steel's board met and appointed John G. A. Leishman (the man with whom Frick had been meeting when Berkman tried to assassinate the industrialist) president of the company. Half of Frick's ownership stake in the company was transferred to Leishman. Freed from his day-to-day responsibilities, Frick was able to devote himself to travel and leisure, and his relationship with Carnegie improved somewhat.

However, all was not well. Despite a 20 percent increase in profits during 1896, Carnegie was unhappy with the new president and forced him out at the end of the year. Leishman was replaced by Charles Schwab, who was promoted from superintendent of Homestead. In his new role, Schwab outshone Leishman, increasing profits by 15 percent in 1897, 160 percent in 1898, and 183 percent in 1899.[11] The explosion of profits made the company, whose stock was undervalued to begin with, all the more attractive. When Carnegie deliberately derailed a plan to sell the company that would have netted Frick a great deal of money, their relationship cooled. The tension was exacerbated by disputes over the price at which Frick would sell coke to Carnegie Steel and over Frick's attempt to sell the company a tract of land he owned near the Homestead works. Carnegie began denigrating Frick behind the chairman's back, and it was not long before the Scot's words reached Frick. However, it was Carnegie's attempt to merge H. C. Frick with Carnegie Steel that really poisoned their relationship. Carnegie had a habit of undervaluing his company's stock, in part to lower payments to stockholders who were forced out of the company. Frick agreed to the merger only if Carnegie agreed to value the new company at $150 million; while this was still lower than the merged companies' estimated value, it would have provided a sizeable windfall for Frick. Carnegie refused, so Frick verbally attacked Carnegie at a Carnegie Steel board meeting. Carnegie retaliated by spreading rumors about Frick's mental health and set about abolishing the position of chairman to force Frick out of the company. The Scot asked Charles Schwab to speak with Frick and convince the chairman to resign. Schwab obliged and was nearly thrown out of Frick's house for the effort, but Carnegie got what he wanted: on December 5, 1899, Frick resigned from the company for the last time.

Unfortunately, this did not end the fireworks. On January 10, 1900, Carnegie dropped by Frick's office and announced that the board had decided to invoke a clause in Frick's contract that forced the now former chairman to sell his stock back to the company. This clause, a standard element in the contracts that Carnegie had signed with all of his partners going back decades, had been used to oust troublesome stockholders by purchasing their shares in the company at a fraction of their true value. In Frick's case, Carnegie offered $1.5 million, approximately one-tenth of the shares' value. Frick became so enraged that he chased Carnegie out of the office, declaring that he would let the courts decide the shares' true value.

In March, Frick sued Carnegie, which frightened the steel baron because such a suit threatened to make the company's financial information public record. As details of the suit began trickling out, Carnegie was besieged by telegrams from industrialists and prominent members of the Republican Party, all of whom urged him to quietly settle the matter lest it cause a scandal that negatively affected the financial markets or the upcoming presidential campaign. As a result, Carnegie caved, and the two companies—Carnegie Steel (valued at $250 million) and H. C. Frick & Company (valued at $70 million)—were merged. Frick received approximately $31 million in cash and interest-bearing bonds in the new company, more than 2,000 percent of the amount Carnegie had originally

J. Pierpont Morgan (1837–1913)

John Pierpont Morgan was an American banker, financier and philanthropist best known for the corporate mergers that resulted in General Electric and U.S. Steel. At one point, Morgan was so powerful and wealthy that he was able to stop the Panic of 1907 before it could turn into an economic depression.

Banking was the Morgan family business; Pierpont's father, Junius Spencer Morgan, had founded J. S. Morgan & Company in 1854. In the early 1860s, Pierpont founded his own firm—J. Pierpont Morgan & Company—and in 1871 he formed Drexel, Morgan & Company with famed Philadelphia banker Anthony J. Drexel. When Drexel died, the firm was renamed J. P. Morgan & Company, and by the turn of the century it was one of the world's best known and most powerful banking firms. Using the company's substantial financial resources, Morgan took over companies and reorganized them in order to make them more profitable; this process came to be known as "Morganization." In addition, Morgan brokered the corporate mergers that led to the creation of U.S. Steel, America's first billion-dollar company.

Because of the firm's size, the federal government twice relied on J. P. Morgan & Company to ameliorate the effects of panics. The first time occurred in 1895 when, due to the Panic of 1893, the U.S. Treasury's gold supplies had dwindled. In a partnership with the Rothschilds (a famous European banking family), J. P. Morgan supplied the Treasury Department with 3.5 million ounces of gold in exchange for a 30-year bond. A little more than a decade later, Morgan again came to the rescue by forming a committee of bankers and corporate leaders; this cabal bought stocks and pressured bankers to rearrange the terms of loans in order to prevent companies from failing. These draconian steps were criticized by the media, but essentially ended the panic and prevented the United States from going into a depression.

offered for the stock. However, the damage had been done, and the two never spoke again. Almost exactly a year after settling with Frick, Carnegie sold the company to financier J. Pierpont Morgan for $480 million; the renamed U.S. Steel became the first billion-dollar company in the world.

Carnegie spent much of the rest of his life trying to downplay the importance of Homestead or shift the blame. Ultimately, the last victim of his deceptions was Carnegie himself. In 1912, while writing his autobiography, which he hoped would forever exonerate him from what happened at Homestead, he had one of the company's executives, Alexander Peacock, spend weeks trying to track down a telegram that he remembered receiving from the workers at Homestead.

Carnegie's autobiography was published posthumously, or after his death.

According to Carnegie's memory, the Homestead strikers had sent him a telegram addressing him as "kind master" and imploring him to "tell us what you wish us to do and we will do it for you." When Peacock was unable to find the telegram, Carnegie pressured him to find employees who would swear to either having seen the telegram or, better still, having sent it, but despite his diligent efforts, Peacock was unable to find anyone who could corroborate Carnegie's memory. Nonetheless, Carnegie used the story anyway because it absolved him (in his mind, anyway) from any guilt and proved, once and for all, that it was Frick and not he who was responsible for the terrible events at Homestead, at least as far as he was concerned.

One important aspect of this telegram is that it explains a great deal about how Carnegie saw himself in relation to his workers. That he believed his workers referred to him as "kind master"—a term that was particularly meaningful for a generation that had fought the Civil War—suggests that Carnegie saw himself as a feudal lord, displaying *noblesse oblige* to the serfs who worked for him. In his autobiography, Carnegie made a statement regarding the strike that bolstered this interpretation. According to him, "[. . .] higher wages to men *who respect their employers and are happy and contented* are a good investment."[12] Put another way, it was not enough for Carnegie that his men exchanged their labor for wages; what he wanted (and what he felt he deserved) was their cheerful deference, their recognition of him as their superior. From his perspective, not only should his workers toil in dangerous and backbreaking jobs 12 hours a day for starvation wages; they should do so with smiles on their faces and thanks in their hearts. This is why Carnegie was never quite able (or willing) to understand why men such as John McLuckie saw the events at Homestead as:

> [. . .] a gigantic conspiracy on the part of this company and their representatives, assisted, aided, and abetted by vicious legislation, to deprive the workmen of their right under the Constitution which this Government guarantees, the right of life, liberty, and pursuit of happiness.[13]

Carnegie ultimately fell back on the tactic he had used throughout his career to deflect criticism: deception. He also claimed in his autobiography that "The policy I pursued in cases of difference with our men was that of patiently waiting, reasoning with them, and showing them that their demands were unfair; but never attempting to employ new men in their places—never."[14] This statement was also untrue, as the events at Homestead show. Carnegie and Frick forced a confrontation with the men and then imported replacement workers to Homestead to break the AAISW's strike. Carnegie may have legitimately believed that "Mr. Carnegie 'takes no man's job,'" as he claimed to a group of workers contemplating a strike, but the events at Homestead tell a different tale.[15]

NOTES

1   Les Standiford, *Meet You in Hell* (New York: Crown, 2005), 228.
2   Standiford, *Meet You In Hell*, 227–250; David Nasaw, *Andrew Carnegie* (New York, NY: The Penguin Press, 2006); and Joseph Frazier Wall, *Andrew Carnegie* (Pittsburgh, PA: University of Pittsburgh Press, 1989), 579.
3   David P. Demarest, Jr., "Introduction," in *"The River Ran Red": Homestead 1892*, Ed. Demarest (Pittsburgh, PA: University of Pittsburgh Press, 1992), viii.
4   Hamlin Garland, "Homestead and Its Perilous Trades: Impressions of a Visit," *McClure's Magazine* vol. III no. 1 (June, 1894), 2–4.
5   Ibid., 18. Emphasis in original.
6   Nasaw, *Andrew Carnegie*, 465.
7   Standiford, *Meet You In Hell*, 232.
8   Edward W. Bemis, "The Homestead Strike," *The Journal of Political Economy*, vol. 2 no. 3 (June, 1894): 369–396. Quoted in Wall, *Andrew Carnegie*, 566.
9   Leon Wolff, *Lockout: The Story of the Homestead Strike of 1892* (New York, NY: Harper & Row, Publishers, 1965), 231.
10 Standiford, *Meet You in Hell*, 243–244.
11 Ibid., 250.
12 Andrew Carnegie, "An Employer's View of the Labor Question," in *The Andrew Carnegie Reader*, Ed. Joseph Frazier Wall (Pittsburgh, PA: University of Pittsburgh Press, 1992), 99. Emphasis mine.
13 "Investigation of the Employment of Pinkerton Detectives in Connection with the Labor Troubles at Homestead, PA" (Washington, DC: Government Printing Office, 1892), 99.
14 Andrew Carnegie, *Autobiography of Andrew Carnegie* (New York, NY: Houghton Mifflin, 1929), 230.
15 Ibid., 249.

Documents

Excerpt from *Autobiography* of *Andrew Carnegie*

The following is an excerpt from Andrew Carnegie's autobiography. Published in 1920, almost 30 years after the events at Homestead, the autobiography was Carnegie's last chance to frame the strike the way he chose to remember it.

[. . .] On July 1, 1892, during my absence in the Highlands of Scotland, there occurred the one really serious quarrel with our workers in our whole history. For twenty-six years I had been actively in charge of the relations between ourselves and our men, and it was the pride of my life to think how delightfully satisfactory these had been and were. I hope I fully deserved what my chief partner, Mr. Phipps, said in his letter to the "New York Herald," January 30, 1904, in reply to one who had declared I had remained abroad during the Homestead strike, instead of flying back to support my partners. It was to the effect that "I was always disposed to yield to the demands of the men, however unreasonable"; hence one or two of my partners did not want me to return. Taking no account of the reward that comes from feeling that you and your employees are friends and judging only from economic results, I believe that higher wages to men who respect their employers and are happy and contented are a good investment, yielding indeed, big dividends.

The manufacture of steel was revolutionized by the Bessemer open-hearth and basic inventions. The machinery hitherto employed had become obsolete, and our firm, recognizing this, spent millions at Homestead reconstructing and enlarging the works. The new machinery made about sixty percent more steel than the old. Two hundred and eighteen tonnage men (that is, men who were paid by the ton of steel produced) were working under a three years' contract, part of the last year being with the new machinery. Thus their earnings had increased almost sixty percent before the end of the contract.

The firm offered to divide this sixty percent with [the men] in the new [pay] scale to be made thereafter. That is to say, the earnings of the men would have been thirty percent greater than under the old scale and the other thirty percent would have gone to the firm to recompense it for the outlay. The work of the men would not have been much harder than it had been hitherto, as the improved machinery did the work. This was not only fair and liberal, it was generous, and under ordinary circumstances it would have been accepted by the men with thanks. But the firm was then engaged in making armor for the United States Government, which we had declined twice to manufacture and which was urgently needed [. . .] Some of the leaders of the men, knowing these conditions, insisted upon demanding the whole sixty percent, thinking the firm would be compelled to give it. The firm could not agree, nor should it have agreed to such an attempt as this to take it by the throat and say, "Stand and deliver." [. . .] Had I been at home nothing would have induced me to yield to this unfair attempt to extort.

[. . .] The policy I had pursued in cases of differences with our men was that of patiently waiting, reasoning with them, and showing them that their demands were unfair; but never attempting to employ new men in their places—never. The superintendent of Homestead, however, was assured by the three thousand men who were not concerned in the dispute that they could run the works, and were anxious to rid themselves of the two hundred and eighteen men who had banded themselves into a union and into which they had hitherto refused to admit those in other departments—only the "heaters" and "rollers" of steel being eligible.

My partners were misled by the superintendent, who was himself misled.

[. . .] It is easy to look back and say that the vital step of opening the works should never have been taken. All the firm had to do was to say to the men: "There is a labor dispute here and you must settle it between yourselves. The firm has made you a most liberal offer. The works will run when the disputed is adjusted, and not till [sic] then. Meanwhile your places remain open to you." [. . .] Instead of this, it was thought advisable (as an additional precaution by the state officials, as I understand) to have the sheriff with guards to protect the thousands against the hundreds. The leaders of the latter were violent and aggressive men; they had guns and pistols, and, as was soon proved, were able to intimidate the thousands.

I quote what I once laid down in writing as our rule: "My idea is that the Company should be known as determined to let the men at any works stop work; that it will confer freely with them and wait patiently

until they decide to return to work, never thinking of trying new men—
never." The best men as men, and the best workmen, are not walking
the streets looking for work. Only the inferior class as a rule is idle. The
kind of men we desired are rarely allowed to lose their jobs, even in dull
times. It is impossible to get new men to run successfully the complicated
machinery of a modern steel plant. The attempt to put in new men
converted the thousands of old men who desired to work, into lukewarm
supporters of our policy, for workmen can always be relied upon to resent
the employment of new men. Who can blame them?

If I had been at home, however, I might have been persuaded to open
the works, as the superintendent desired, to test whether our old men would
go to work as they had promised. But it should be noted that the works
were not opened at first by my partners for new men. On the contrary,
it was, as I was informed upon my return, at the wish of the thousands of
our old men that they were opened. This is a vital point. My partners were
in no way blamable for making the trial so recommended by the superintendent. Our rule never to employ new men, but to wait for the old to
return, had not been violated so far. In regard to the second opening of the
works, after the strikers had shot at the sheriff's officers, it is also easy to
look back and say, "How much better had the works been closed until the
old men voted to return"; but the Governor of Pennsylvania, with eight
thousand troops, had meanwhile taken charge of the situation.

I was travelling in the Highlands of Scotland when the trouble arose,
and did not hear of it until two days after. Nothing I have ever had to
meet in all my life, before or since, wounded me so deeply. No pangs
remain of any wound received in my business career save that of
Homestead. It was so unnecessary. The men were outrageously wrong.
The strikers, with the new machinery, would have made from four to
nine dollars a day under the new scale—thirty percent more than they
were making with the old machinery. While in Scotland I received the
following cable from the officers of the union of our workmen:

"Kind master, tell us what you wish us to do and we shall do it
for you."

This was most touching, but, alas, too late. The mischief was done,
the works were in the hands of the Governor; it was too late.

I received, while abroad, numerous kind messages from friends
conversant with the circumstances, who imagined my unhappiness. The
following from Mr. Gladstone was greatly appreciated:

MY DEAR MR. CARNEGIE,

My wife has long ago offered her thanks, with my own, for your most
kind congratulations. But I do not forget that you have been suffering

yourself from anxieties, and have been exposed to imputations in connection with your gallant efforts to direct rich men into a course of action more enlightened than that which they usually follow. I wish I could relieve you from these imputations of journalists, too often rash, conceited or censorious, rancorous, ill-natured. I wish to do the little, the very little, that is in my power, which is simply to say how sure I am that no one who knows you will be prompted by the unfortunate occurrences across the water (of which manifestly we cannot know the exact merits) to qualify in the slightest degree either his confidence in your generous views or his admiration of the good and great work you have already done.

Wealth is at present like a monster threatening to swallow up the moral life of man; you by precept and by example have been teaching him to disgorge. I for one thank you.

Believe me.

Very faithfully yours,

(Signed) W. E. Gladstone

I insert this as giving proof, if proof were needed, of Mr. Gladstone's large, sympathetic nature, alive and sensitive to everything transpiring of a nature to arouse sympathy—Neopolitans, Greeks, and Bulgarians one day, or a stricken friend the next.

The general public, of course, did not know that I was in Scotland and knew nothing of the initial trouble at Homestead. Workmen had been killed at the Carnegie Works, of which I was controlling owner. That was sufficient to make my name a by-word for years. But at last some satisfaction came. Senator Hanna was president of the National Civic Federation, a body composed of capitalists and workmen which exerted a benign influence over both employers and employed, and the Honorable Oscar Straus, who was then vice-president, invited me to dine at his house and meet officials of the Federation. Before the date appointed Mark Hanna, its president, my lifelong friend and former agent at Cleveland, had suddenly passed away. I attended the dinner. At its close Mr. Straus arose and said that the question of a successor to Mr. Hanna had been considered, and he had to report that every labor organization heard from had favored me for the position. There were present several of the labor leaders who, one after another, arose and corroborated Mr. Straus.

I do not remember so complete a surprise and, I shall confess, one so grateful to me. That I deserved well from labor I felt. I knew myself to be warmly sympathetic with the working-man, and also thought that I had the regard of our workmen; but throughout the country it was naturally the reverse, owing to the Homestead riot. The Carnegie Works meant to the public Mr. Carnegie's war upon labor's just earnings.

[. . .] A mass meeting of the workmen and their wives was afterwards held in the Library Hall at Pittsburgh to greet me, and I addressed them from both my head and my heart. The one sentence I remember, and always shall, was to the effect that capital, labor, and employer were a three-legged stool, none before or after all the others, all equally indispensible. Then came the cordial handshaking and all was well. Having thus rejoined hands and hearts with our employees and their wives, I felt that a great weight had been effectually lifted, but I had had a terrible experience although thousands of miles from the scene.

An incident flowing from the Homestead trouble is told by my friend, Professor John C. Van Dyke, of Rutgers College.

In the spring of 1900, I went up from Guymas, on the Gulf of California, to the ranch of a friend at La Noria Verde, thinking to have a week's shooting in the mountains of Sonora. The ranch was far enough removed from civilization, and I had expected meeting there only a few Mexicans and many Yaqui Indians, but much to my surprise I found an English-speaking man, who proved to be an American. I did not have long to wait in order to find out what brought him there, for he was lonesome and disposed to talk. His name was McLuckie, and up to 1892 he had been a skilled mechanic in the employ of the Carnegie Steel Works at Homestead. He was what was called a "top hand," received large wages, was married, and at that time had a home and considerable property. In addition, he had been honored by his fellow-townsmen and had been made burgomaster of Homestead.

When the strike of 1892 came McLuckie naturally sided with the strikers, and in his capacity as burgomaster gave the order to arrest the Pinkerton detectives who had come to Homestead by steamer to protect the works and preserve order. He believed he was fully justified in doing this. As he explained it to me, the detectives were an armed force invading his bailiwick, and he had a right to arrest and disarm them. The order led to bloodshed, and the conflict was begun in real earnest.

The story of the strike is, of course, well known to all. The strikers were finally defeated. As for McLuckie, he was indicted for murder, riot, treason, and I know not what other offense. He was compelled to flee the State, was wounded, starved, pursued by the officers of the law, and obliged to go into hiding until the storm blew over. Then he found he was blacklisted by all the steel men in the United States and could not get employment anywhere. His money was gone, and, as a final blow, his wife died and his home was broken up. After many vicissitudes he resolved to go to Mexico, and at the time I met him he was trying to get employment in the mines about fifteen miles from La Noria Verde. But he was too good a mechanic for the Mexicans, who required in mining the cheapest kind of unskilled peon labor. He could get nothing to do and had no money. He was literally down to his last copper. Naturally, as he told the story of his misfortunes, I felt very sorry for him, especially as he was a most intelligent person and did no unnecessary whining about his troubles.

I do not think I told him at the time that I knew Mr. Carnegie and had been with him at Cluny in Scotland shortly after the Homestead strike, nor that I knew from Mr. Carnegie the other side of the story. But McLuckie was rather careful not to blame Mr. Carnegie, saying to me several times that if "Andy" had been there the trouble would never have arisen. He seemed to think "the boys" could get on very well with "Andy" but not so well with some of his partners.

I was at the ranch for a week and saw a good deal of McLuckie in the evenings. When I left there, I went directly to Tucson, Arizona, and from there I had occasion to write to Mr. Carnegie, and in the letter I told him about the meeting with McLuckie. I added that I felt very sorry for the man and thought that he had been treated rather badly. Mr. Carnegie answered at once, and on the margin of the letter wrote in lead pencil: "Give McLuckie all the money he wants, but don't mention my name." I wrote to McLuckie immediately, offering him what money he needed, mentioning no sum, but giving him to understand that it would be sufficient to put him on his feet again. He declined it. He said he would fight it out and make his own way, which was the right-enough American spirit. I could not help but admire it in him.

As I remember it now, I spoke about him later to a friend, Mr. J. A. Naugle, the general manager of the Sonora Railway. At any rate, McLuckie got a job with the railway at driving wells, and made a great success of it. A year later, or perhaps it was in the autumn of the same year, I again met him at the Guaymas, where he was superintending some repairs on his machinery at the railway shops. He was much changed for the better, seemed happy, and to add to his contentment, had taken unto himself a Mexican wife. And now that his sky cleared, I was anxious to tell him the truth about my offer that he might not think unjustly of those who had been compelled to fight him. So before I left, I said,

"McLuckie, I want you to know now that the money I offered you was not mine. That was Andrew Carnegie's money. It was his offer, made through me."

McLuckie was fairly stunned, and all he could say was:

"Well, that was damned white of Andy, wasn't it?"

I would rather risk that verdict of McLuckie's as a passport to Paradise than all the theological dogmas invented by man. I knew McLuckie well as a good fellow. It was said his property in Homestead was worth thirty thousand dollars. He was under arrest for the shooting of the police officers because he was burgomaster, and also the chairman of the Men's Committee of Homestead. He had to fly, leaving all behind him.

Source: Andrew Carnegie, "The Homestead Strike," *Autobiography of Andrew Carnegie* (New York, NY: Houghton Mifflin Company, 1920), 228–238.

"Tyrant Frick"

In the days and weeks following the violence at Homestead, many American newspapers published editorials, political cartoons, and even songs about the events that rocked Western Pennsylvania. This song, from the National Labor Tribune, a pro-labor newspaper published in Pittsburgh, provides the workingmen's perspective on the Homestead Strike.

In days gone by before the war
    All freemen did agree
The best of plans to handle slaves
    Was to let them all go free;
But the slave-drivers then, like now,
    Continued to make a kick
And keep the slaves in bondage tight,
    Just like our Tyrant Frick.

CHORUS:
Of all slave-drivers, for spite and kick,
No one so cruel as Tyrant Frick.

The brave Hungarians, sons of toil,
    When seeking which was right,
Were killed like dogs by tyrants' hands
    In the coke districts' fight.
Let labor heroes all be true—
    Avenge the *bloody trick*!
Be firm like steel, true to the cause,
    And conquer Tyrant Frick.

CHORUS:
Of all slave-drivers, for spite and kick,
No one so cruel as Tyrant Frick.

The traitorous Pinkerton low tribe,
    In murdering attack,
Tried hard to take our lives and homes,
    But heroes drove them back.
O! sons of toil, o'er all the land,
    Now hasten, and be quick
To aid us, in our efforts grand,
    To down this Tyrant Frick.

CHORUS:
Of all slave-drivers, for spite and kick,
No one so cruel as Tyrant Frick.

The battle of "Fort Frick" is stamped
    On page of history,
And marked with blood of freemen true,
    Against this tyranny!
The sons of toil, for ages to come,
    His curse will always bring;
The name of *Frick* will be well known—
    The Nigger driver King!

CHORUS:
Of all slave-drivers, for spite and kick,
No one so cruel as Tyrant Frick.

Source: Anonymous, "Tyrant Frick," *National Labor Tribune* (Pittsburgh,
PA, August 27, 1892).

DOCUMENT 3

Testimony of Henry Clay Frick

Unlike Carnegie, Frick never published an autobiography, so his testimony before the House Committee on the Judiciary's investigation into the events at Homestead provides one of the one of the few instances where he publicly expressed his side of the story. The following is an excerpt that details Frick's actions in the days leading up to the Pinkertons' attempt to occupy the Homestead works.

THE CHAIRMAN

Q. Now, Mr. Frick, will you state what was proposed by your company to these laborers which they rejected?—A. Well, if you will permit me, I would like to say that in January last year we tried to take up question with the Amalgamated Association at Homestead, to arrange for a new scale to take the place of the one expiring on the 30th of June of this year. We had some difficulty in getting them to take the question up, and did not succeed in getting them to do so until March. They then presented a scale—

Q. Let me interrupt you there. You say that you mean all the workmen?—A. The Amalgamated men at Homestead.

Q. What is the name?—A. The Amalgamated Association of Iron and Steel Workers.

Q. To them you made a proposition?—A. Yes, sir. They, in March, presented a scale covering almost all the departments at Homestead, and in almost every instance it called for an advance in wages. We had several conferences with them there at that time, and up until almost the 30th of May, [we were unable] to reach any understanding when we prepared the scales covering four departments at those works [. . .]

Q. Well, what next?—A. A committee, said to be from the Homestead Steel Works, called at our office at about 10 o'clock on the 23rd of June.

We opened the discussion first by asking what they had to say. We then discussed the minimum, the proposed change to the minimum, that is, in the price of billets. They argued that there should be no reduction in the minimum. They could not agree to accept anything below $25. I told them I did not understand why there should be any minimum, as there was no maximum. We were willing to pay as they went up; they ought to be willing to accept a reduction as they declined, for the reason that when billets go down to 21 and 22 there was no money in it to us, and we would only be operating the mill in order to keep up our organization and give employment to our workmen [. . .]

I left the room. Mr. Potter, our general superintendent, remained behind, and, as I learned afterwards, invited Mr. Weihe and some of the committee to remain, and discussed the matter with them for a while, and said he would endeavor to persuade us to increase the minimum that we had offered $1 per ton, making 23. They agreed to let him come and see me and see what we could agree to, which he did, and I told him we did not want to be arbitrary; we wanted to be liberal and we would agree to that—to increase the minimum to 23, asking only a reduction of $2 from the minimum of the previous scale. Those of the committee who had remained left Mr. Potter and said they would go and see their men and call at a later hour and give their report. They called at a later hour and said their men would not agree to it. That is the only conference we have had.

Q. What followed that?—A. The works continued in operation until, I think, the 29th or the 30th, when they were closed down.

Q. The 29th or 30th of June?—A. Yes, sir [. . .]

Q. Mr. Frick, you stated that after the sheriff had gone out with a small posse that you then employed these Pinkertons because you knew of no other way of producing a guard for your property. Did you make any effort? Did the sheriff make any application to the governor of the State for troops to enable him to restore possession of your property to you?—A. That is before we brought those guards.

Q. Before?—A. I will tell you how those guards happened to be brought; that is what you want.

Q. Yes, sir.—A. As I stated in my interview, the experience of three years ago convinced us beyond a doubt that the sheriff of this county was powerless to give us the protection which we should have; so we concluded that we would obtain watchmen of our own, pay them ourselves, put them on our own property, have them remain on our own property, not to go outside of it or off of it. I then had preliminary arrangements made for these men with an agent of Mr. Pinkerton, that is to say, an understanding what we would pay for these men [. . .]

Q. You were anticipating trouble?—A. Yes, sir; judging from the experience we had three years ago.

MR. BOATNER

Q. What notice had you at the time you wrote the letter [to the Pinkerton Detective Agency arranging for 300 Pinkerton agents] that there would be any attempt by the Amalgamated Association to prevent you from operating your property in your own way?—A. The experience we had three years ago. And [the Pinkerton agents] were subject to recall at any time if we found they were not needed.

Q. Had anything been said or done by your employees at Homestead, which notified you of their intention to forcibly prevent you from operating the mills at the time you wrote the letter?—A. I cannot say it was anything special except that we knew their tactics.

THE CHAIRMAN

Q. After shutting down your mills did you have a plank stockade erected around your property?— A. We had the works fenced in; that has been going on for over a month past; and something we have had in contemplation for a long while.

Q. Was it in consideration of trouble that you might have with the workmen?—A. That had something to do with it; yes, sir.

Q. Was it not done for the purpose of putting the property in a position that it could be more easily defended against an assault?—A. Yes, sir; that is correct.

Source: "Testimony of Henry Clay Frick," *Investigation of the Employment of Pinkerton Detectives in Connection with the Labor Troubles at Homestead, PA* (Washington, DC: U.S. Government Printing Office, 1892), 22–34.

Testimony of Hugh O'Donnell

*T*his document, and the one that follows it, details the experiences of two key strikers: Hugh O'Donnell and John McLuckie. In the paragraphs that follow, O'Donnell provides a firsthand account of the Pinkertons' attempts to land at Homestead.

THE CHAIRMAN

Q. After the shut down of the mills did the workmen who had been employed theretofore exercise any control over them in respect to keeping anybody out and looking after the property or any sort of supervision, and, if so, to what extent within your observation?—A. To this extent, that there was a mass meeting held, and there was quite a large number there. For instance, there was a mechanical department there, that is mechanics, blacksmiths, and others who are purely incidental to the production of a ton of steel and we called a mass meeting.

Q. They were not affected by this?—A. No; they were not affected by the scale at all. We called a mass meeting and we considered the matter, and a resolution was passed there that they remain out with us until such time as we arrived at an agreement with the firm. Immediately after the mass meeting all the lodges—the meetings are secret to a certain extent, as all business transactions are mostly—the eight lodges had a joint meeting and they deliberated upon the crisis at hand and they elected a certain number from each lodge—assuming they had the responsibility, each of the eight lodges was empowered to appoint five members to an advisory committee. Then this action was taken. Members were appointed to this committee by each lodge. I was appointed our president, with several others, and we organized ourselves into an advisory committee and I was elected chairman of that. The advisory committee got headquarters. We knew if we went on strike there we had quite a number of irresponsible people and there would be others coming from a distance, and we appointed subcommittees and we placed men around the works to guard them; not around the fence, but on the outside to keep outsiders, wholly irresponsible people, from doing any damage.

Q. You placed them outside of the fence which had been placed around the works of the company?—A. Yes, sir.

Q. When was that done, on what date?—A. I do not remember the date but I think it must have been on the 30th of June or on the 1st of July. The 1st of July, I think it was, that the mass meeting was called and that committee was organized, but these men were fully instructed they should simply use moral suasion, and that nobody should be threatened, that there should be no violent language. We did that because we assumed we had the moral responsibility and each man pledged himself. The best men, in my estimate, composed each advisory committee, that is, sober men.

Q. They were instructed to keep men from entering the works?—A. No, sir; I will say positively not.

Q. They were instructed to keep out intruders; if they were not instructed to keep anyone out, what were they put there for?—A. They were put there to prevail on anyone who felt inclined to go in. We had an intimation that quite a number of men had been hired in the East, although we had no evidence of that, and we thought if they encountered those people they could persuade them to remain out until such time as the men and the firm could have an agreement.

Q. Nonunion men?—A. Yes, sir.

Q. They were there to use moral suasion with such people who came to keep them from going into the works in the employ of the company?—A. Yes, sir.

Q. And they were not there for the purpose of using any violence?—A. No, sir; their methods were peaceable [. . .]

Q. If you were there and saw [the events at Homestead on July 6, 1892] we would like to hear from you, as you are an intelligent man?—A. Thank you.

Q. We would like to hear from you because you can give the details probably much better than some other witnesses can?—A. Well, I am going to make a brief statement regarding the matter. I could not say the exact hour, but I think the alarm came up about 2 o'clock or 3 that two barges loaded with Pinkertons were coming up the river. That was the alarm spread out which aroused the entire population. I, with others, got out of bed and with Capt. Coon, who was a near neighbor of mine, we both went down to the river bank and there had already assembled a very large crowd of people—men, women, and children. There were a lot of half-grown boys and there were Slavs, Hungarians, and others who were firing pistols in the air. They must have been firing in the air because Capt. Coon and another man were passing along the crowd and were admonishing the crowd to stop this firing of pistols and put them back in their pockets. We were going along with the crowd, following the crowd, and there had been a few random shots, but whether they were fired at the boat or not I could not say. I was on the edge of the river bank and I had my hands up advising the men not to fire, but who they were I could not answer. It was dusky and there was a fog on the river.

Q. It was early in the morning?—A. Yes, sir; I with others followed the crowd up the river to the landing. They had broken down some of the boards, that is, the fence belonging to the boundary limits of the city farm, the borough limits, and pulled down several boards, I do not know how many, and we passed through there and went to the river bank and saw them land. Capt. Coon and I and another friend who accompanied us went down close to the beach, and there was quite an excited crowd standing around them and they were hallooing to the captain to pull back and not to land. I do not know how it came about, but there was some scuffle around the gangplank; I stood with my back to the beach about 40 feet, as I showed you yesterday, and there was some firing. I did not see any rifles in the congregation on the river bank and I saw no one, but I think I heard a rifle shot and then a regular volley at that. I was still addressing the crowd. One ball crossed my thumb [holding up same]—it is nearly well now—and struck another man in the head and I crawled up the bank and got behind a sewer trap until the fire ceased, which I should say was about five minutes' duration [. . .]

Q. Could you state whether the shots were fired from the people on the shore at the men on the barges or boats first or did the men on the barges and boats fire first?—A. I cannot answer that question. That is, when they were coming along the river?

Q. Or when they attempted to land?—A. I do not think there was a shot fired from the crowd until they fired into it, but there was one rifle shot and a volley, but where that came from I do not know. I was informed there was a man attempting to move the gang plank there, at whom it was fired.

Q. You need not state that, but just what you saw and know of your own knowledge. How long did the fight continue; you came out of the sewer trap after awhile?—A. Yes, sir, after they ceased firing.

Source: "Testimony of Hugh O'Donnell," *Investigation of the Employment of Pinkerton Detectives in Connection with the Labor Troubles at Homestead, PA* (Washington, DC: U.S. Government Printing Office, 1892), 88–91.

Testimony of John McLuckie

L *ike Hugh O'Donnell, striker John McLuckie also testified to the committee during the House's investigation into the events at Homestead. As you can see from the short excerpt that follows, McLuckie's tone is quite different from O'Donnell's and his version of the events leading up to the strike is quite different from Frick's.*

THE CHAIRMAN

Q. What points were involved in the proposition wherein it differed from the contract under which you were at work?—A. From what information I received from the sources I have mentioned I think that there were three points involved; that is what I understood from our committee. One is the change in the minimum, another is the change of the time for the expiration of the scale, and another is a reduction in wages.

Q. Do you know about the time when the mills were shut down?— A. Yes, sir.

Q. When was that?—A. We shut down on the 29th of June; that is, the converting department.

Q. The one in which you worked shut down on the 29th of June?— A. Yes, sir.

Q. That was the consequence of a disagreement between the company and certain employees?—A. I so understood.

Q. Do you know anything of any trouble which resulted subsequently from attempts to put Pinkerton guards in possession of the mill?—A. I heard there was some trouble.

Q. You did not witness any?—A. No, sir; I am burgess of that borough, I am the peace officer.

Q. You were there on the morning of the 6th of July when this trouble or this fight occurred?—A. At Homestead?

Q. Yes, sir.—A. Yes, sir.

Q. Did you see anything or know anything of it of your own knowledge?—A. I saw them carrying the dead and wounded back into the town and supposed that there might be a conflict about the mill or somewhere else. I could not locate it at the time.

Q. You did not see anything of that?—A. Not of the conflict; no, sir.

Q. Is there anything else you wish to state of your own knowledge?—A. I do not know—

Q. Connected with this trouble between the company and the employees?—A. I do not know that there is anything that would be of interest to this committee. I should prefer the committee ask me anything they think proper. However, I want to go on record to this effect that I think it was a gigantic conspiracy on the part of this company and their representatives, assisted, aided, and abetted by vicious legislation, to deprive the workmen of their right under the Constitution which the Government guarantees, the right of life and liberty in pursuit of happiness. I think that is a fact and if the opportunity was afforded I supposed we could establish that [. . .]

MR. TAYLOR

[. . .] A. In regard to giving you a better idea of the Pinkertons, I do not wish this little affair at Homestead to be considered a war between labor and capital. That was a war, if it could be so styled, between laboring men because these Pinkertons and their associates were there under a consideration they were there under pay, and the person who employed that force was safely placed away by the money that he has wrung from the sweat of the men employed in that mill, employing in their stead workmen to go there and kill the men who made his money.

Source: "Testimony of John McLuckie," *Investigation of the Employment of Pinkerton Detectives in Connection with the Labor Troubles at Homestead, PA* (Washington, DC: U.S. Government Printing Office, 1892), 98–105.

Newspaper coverage of Homestead

During the late nineteenth century, most newspapers were quite partisan, which often affected the tone of their news coverage. The selections that follow are taken from a broad range of local and national newspapers to illustrate the fact that people who witnessed the events at Homestead drew vastly different conclusions about those events.

AT WAR!

Homestead, Pa., July 6.—A bloody battle has taken place between the workmen locked out of Andrew Carnegie's mill and 300 Pinkerton men sent from Pittsburg to invest the works.

The fight occurred at daylight at the steamboat landing near the mills, where the workmen were massed to prevent the officers from landing.

The detectives, according to the statements of several witnesses, began hostilities by opening fire with Winchesters on the men.

The fire was returned from revolvers and shotguns, and the workmen made so determined a resistance that the officers were unable to land [. . .]

Source: "At War!" *Evening World* (New York, NY, July 6, 1892), 1.

LIKE RATS IN A TRAP

One of the most graphic narratives of the experience of the men on the barges was related last evening by A. L. Wells, a student at the Bennett Medical College, of Chicago.

He came down with six wounded Pinkerton men who were brought to the Union station at 7:10 last evening [. . .]

He was elated over his escape from the mob, and was a willing talker.

"I was sent on here by the Pinkertons," he began. "They told 124 of us who left Chicago that we were wanted as private watchmen. They expected us to get inside the works, and then if we were besieged and any were injured I was to take care of them. The men who came on are not regular employees of the Pinkertons, but were picked up at random."

"Long before we arrived at Homestead the firing commenced, and the bullets were dropping all around us, but until we got within easy gunshot no bullets struck the barges. It then began to dawn upon the men that there was serious trouble ahead, and we began to prepare for a systematic defense."

"When the steamboat left us the bullets flew around like a perfect hail storm and pattered against us from every side. For a short time the men with the guns made an attempt to return the fire but after 10 or 12 of our party had been wounded we gave it up as a bad job."

"The groans and curses of the wounded mingled with the prayers and pleadings of the dying, as they laid in the bottom of the barges; the whistle and ring of bullets; the reports of the guns, and the shouts of caution, formed a scene of indescribable horror. It was a terrible experience, and one that blanched the cheek of the most fearless."

"We were caged like rats in a trap. The situation was desperate. The chances were 100 to 1 that not a man of us would get out alive. After we had run up a flag of truce for the third time, and each time it had been shot down, we gave up all hope. The dynamite bombs thrown at us blew out one side of a barge as though it were paper, and I saw men in the party who were contemplating suicide in preference to enduring the horrible strain, which would undoubtedly end only in death if no mercy had been shown us. If we had known the awful treatment which we were subsequently let to undergo, it is a question where the men would have capitulated when they did."

"We relied implicitly upon the word of the leaders to give us protection, but instead all but a few of the wounded were tortured worse than if they had fallen into the hands of savages. Even some of the men who were injured were kicked and beaten into insensibility. It was a sickening sight, brutal and barbarous to a degree almost past belief. I never imagined that such scenes could be enacted in a community of civilized men."

Source: "Like Rats in a Trap," *Pittsburg Dispatch* (Pittsburgh, PA, July 7, 1892), 2.

CIVIL WAR: CARNEGIE'S EFFORTS TO CRUSH
ORGANIZED LABOR RESULTS IN CIVIL WAR

Homestead, July 6.—[Special.]—Civil war at Homestead. Excitement intense. Two men dead. Many others wounded. What will the end be? No one can tell. Shall organized labor be crushed by Pinkerton detectives armed with Winchester rifles. This is a question to be settled [. . .]

At 4:30 this morning 300 Pinkerton detectives landed from barges at the Homestead Steel Works of Carnegie & Co. Immediately 5,000 strikers broke over the fences and charged upon the invaders. The men were heavily armed and firing began at once. The Pinkertons were forced to retreat to their boats. There was no chance of telling how many were killed or wounded, but the volleys from each side were heavy and bodies of dead and wounded were carried out of the enclosure of the works to a house near by [. . .] The Pinkerton men were secured by the firm after the deputy sheriffs had been run away Tuesday evening [. . .]

Chairman Frick, of the Carnegie Company, again refused today to confer with his lockedout men at Homestead. The report that the Pinkertons had withdrawn, was untrue. The boat that came to this city brought a number of the injured and returned to Homewood [*sic*] at once [. . .]

The trouble at Homestead causes great excitement in political circles [in Washington]. The Democrats will appoint a Congressional committee to investigate and make a report. [Pennsylvania Senator Matthew S.] Quay advises Pattison to try and settle the trouble without using the troops.

Source: "CIVIL WAR: Carnegie's Efforts to Crush Organized Labor Results in Civil War," *Stark County Democrat* (Canton, OH, July 7, 1892), 5.

DOCUMENT 7

Excerpt from *Prison Memoirs of an Anarchist*

After trying to assassinate Frick, Berkman served 14 years in Pittsburgh's notorious Western State Penitentiary. Upon his release, he wrote his memoirs in which he sought to explain and justify his attempt to kill Frick. "The Girl" to whom Berkman refers is his lover, anarchist Emma Goldman. Her memories of these events follow in the next document.

Clearly, every detail of that day is engraved on my mind. It is the sixth of July, 1892. We are quietly sitting in the back of our little flat—Fedya and I—when suddenly the Girl enters. Her naturally quick, energetic steps more than usually resolute. As I turn to her, I am struck by the peculiar gleam in her eyes and the heightened color.

"Have you read it?" she cries, waving the half-open newspaper.

"What is it?"

"Homestead. Strikers shot. Pinkertons have killed women and children."

She speaks in a quick, jerky manner. Her words ring like the cry of a wounded animal, the melodious voice tinged with the harshness of bitterness—the bitterness of helpless agony.

I take the newspaper from her hands. In growing excitement I read the vivid account of the tremendous struggle, the Homestead strike, or, more correctly, the lockout. The report details the conspiracy on the part of the Carnegie Company to crush the Amalgamated Association of Iron and Steel Workers; the selection, for the purpose, of Henry Clay Frick, whose attitude toward labor is implacably hostile; his secret military preparations while designedly prolonging the peace negotiations with the Amalgamated; the fortification of the Homestead steel-works; the erection of a high board fence, capped by barbed wire and provided with loopholes for sharpshooters; the hiring of an army of Pinkerton thugs; the attempt to smuggle them, in the dead of night, into Homestead; and, finally, the terrible carnage.

I pass the paper to Fedya. The Girl glances at me. We sit in silence, each busy with his own thoughts. Only now and then we exchange a word, a searching, significant look.

[. . .] The great battle has been fought. Never before, in all its history, has American labor won such a signal victory. By force of arms the workers of Homestead have compelled three hundred Pinkerton invaders to surrender, to surrender most humbly, ignominiously. What humiliating defeat for the powers that be! Does not the Pinkerton janizary represent organized authority, forever crushing the toiler in the interest of the exploiters? Well may the enemies of the People be terrified at the unexpected awakening. But the People, the workers of America, have joyously acclaimed the rebellious manhood of Homestead. The steel-workers were not the aggressors. Resignedly they had toiled and suffered. Out of their flesh and bone grew the great steel industry; on their blood fattened the powerful Carnegie corporation. Yet patiently they had waited for the promised greater share of the wealth they were creating. Like a bolt from a clear sky came the blow: wages were to be reduced!

[. . .] With smooth words the great philanthropist had persuaded the workers to indorse the high steel tariff. Every product of his mills protected, Andrew Carnegie secured a reduction in the duty on steel billets, in return for his generous contribution to the Republican campaign fund. In complete control of the billet market, the Carnegie firm engineered a depression of prices, as a seeming consequence of a lower duty. *But the market price of billets was the sole standard of wages in the Homestead mills.* The wages of the workers must be reduced! The offer of the Amalgamated Association to arbitrate the new scale met with contemptuous refusal: there was nothing to arbitrate; the men must submit unconditionally; the union was to be exterminated. And Carnegie selected Henry Clay Frick, the bloody Frick of the coke regions, to carry the program into execution.

Must the oppressed forever submit? The manhood of Homestead rebelled: the millmen scorned the despotic ultimatum. Then Frick's hand fell. The war was on! Indignation swept the country. Throughout the land the tyrannical attitude of the Carnegie Company was bitterly denounced, the ruthless brutality of Frick universally execrated.

I could no longer remain indifferent. The moment was urgent. The toilers of Homestead had defied the oppressor. They were awakening. But as yet the steel-workers were only blindly rebellious. The vision of Anarchism alone could imbue discontent with conscious revolutionary purpose; it alone could lend wings to the aspirations of labor. The dissemination of our ideas among the proletariat of Homestead would illumine the great struggle, help to clarify the issues, and point the way to complete ultimate emancipation.

My days were feverish with anxiety. The stirring call, "Labor, Awaken!" would fire the hearts of the disinherited, and inspire them to noble deeds. It would carry to the oppressed the message of the New Day, and prepare them for the approaching Social Revolution. Homestead might prove the first blush of the glorious Dawn. How I chafed at the obstacles my project encountered! Unexpected difficulties impeded every step. The efforts to get the leaflet translated into popular English proved unavailing. It would endanger me to distribute such a fiery appeal, as my friend remonstrated. Impatiently I cast aside his objections. As if personal considerations could for an instant be weighed in the scale of the great Cause! But in vain I argued and pleaded. And all the while precious moments were being wasted, and new obstacles barred the way. I rushed frantically from printer to compositor, begging, imploring. None dared print the appeal. And time was fleeting. Suddenly flashed the news of the Pinkerton carnage. The world stood aghast.

The time for speech was past. Throughout the land the toilers echoed the defiance of the men of Homestead. The steel-workers had rallied bravely to the defence; the murderous Pinkertons were driven from the city. But loudly called the blood of Mammon's victims on the banks of the Monongahela. Loudly it calls. It is the People calling. Ah, the People! The grand, mysterious, yet so near and real, People [. . .]

In my mind I see myself back in the little Russian college town, amid the circle of Petersburg students, home for their vacation, surrounded by the halo of that vague and wonderful something we called "Nihilist." The rushing train, Homestead, the five years passed in America, all turn into a mist, hazy with the distance of unreality, of centuries; and again I sit among the superior beings, reverently listening to the impassioned discussion of dimly understood high themes, with the oft-recurring refrain of "Barzov, Hegel, Liberty, Chernishevsky, v narod." To the People! To the beautiful, simple People so noble in spite of centuries of brutalizing suffering! Like a clarion call the note rings in my ears, amidst the din of contending views and obscure phraseology. The People! My Greek mythology moods have often pictured HIM to me as the mighty Atlas, supporting on his shoulders the weight of the world, his back bent, his face the mirror of unutterable misery, in his eye the look of hopeless anguish, the dumb, pitiful appeal for help. Ah, to help this helplessly suffering giant, to lighten his burden! The way is obscure, the means uncertain, but in the heated student debate the note rings clear: To the People, become one of them, share their joys and sorrows, and thus you will teach them. Yes, that is the solution. But what is that red-headed

Misha from Odessa saying? "It is all good and well about going to the People, but the energetic men of the deed, the Rakhmetovs, blaze the path of popular revolution by the individual acts of revolt against."

"Ticket, please!" A heavy hand is on my shoulder. With an effort I realize the situation. The card-players are exchanging angry words. With a deft movement the conductor unhooks the board, and calmly walks away with it under his arm. A roar of laughter greets the players. Twitted by the other passengers, they soon subside, and presently the car grows quiet.

I have difficulty in keeping myself from falling back into reverie. I must form a definite plan of action. My purpose is quite clear to me. A tremendous struggle is taking place at Homestead: the People are manifesting the right spirit in resisting tyranny and invasion. My heart exults. This is, at last, what I have always hoped for from the American workingmen: once aroused, he will brook no interference; he will fight all obstacles, and conquer even more than his original demands. It is the spirit of the heroic past reincarnated in the steel-workers of Homestead, Pennsylvania. What supreme joy to aid in this work! That is my natural mission. I feel the strength of a great undertaking. No shadow of doubt crosses my mind. The People—the toilers of the world, the producers—comprise, to me, the universe. They alone count. The rest are parasites, who have no right to exist. But to the People belongs the earth—by right, if not in fact. To make it so in fact, all means are justifiable; nay, advisable, even to the point of taking life. The question of moral right in such matters often agitated the revolutionary circles I used to frequent. I had always taken the extreme view. The more radical the treatment, I held, the quicker the cure. Society is a patient; sick constitutionally and functionally. Surgical treatment is often imperative. The removal of a tyrant is not merely justifiable; it is the highest duty of every true revolutionist. Human life is, indeed, sacred and inviolate. But the killing of a tyrant, of an enemy of the People, is in no way considered as the taking of a life. A revolutionist would rather perish a thousand times than be guilty of what is ordinarily called murder. In truth, murder and *Attentat* are to me opposite terms. To remove a tyrant is an act of liberation, the giving of life and opportunity to an oppressed people. True, the Cause often calls upon the revolutionist to commit an unpleasant act; but it is the test of a true revolutionist— nay, more, his pride—to sacrifice all merely human feeling at the call of the People's Cause. If the latter demand his life, so much the better.

Could anything be nobler than to die for a grand, a sublime Cause? Why, the very life of a true revolutionist has not other purpose, no significance whatever, save to sacrifice it on the altar of the beloved People. And what could be higher in life than a true revolutionist? It is to be a *man*, a complete MAN. A being who has neither personal interests nor desires above the necessities of the Cause; one who has emancipated himself from being merely human, and has risen above that, even to the height of conviction which excludes all doubt, all regret; in short, one who in the very inmost of his soul feels himself revolutionist first, human afterwards.

[. . .] At this moment I realize, as perhaps never before, the great joy, the surpassing gladness, of being. But in a trice the picture changes. Before my eyes rises the Monongahela river, carrying barges filled with armed men. And I hear a shot. A boy falls to the gangplank. The blood gushes from the centre of his forehead. The hole ploughed by the bullet yawns black on the crimson face. Cries and wailing ring in my ears. I see men running toward the river, and women kneeling by the side of the dead.

[. . .] "Pitt-s-burgh! Pitt-s-burgh!"

The harsh cry of the conductor startles me with the violence of a shock. Impatient as I am of the long journey, the realization that I have reached my destination comes unexpectedly, overwhelming me with the dread of unpreparedness. In a flurry I gather up my things, but, noticing that the other passengers keep their places, I precipitously resume my seat, fearful lest my agitation be noticed. To hide my confusion, I turn to the open window. Thick clouds of smoke overcast the sky, shrouding the morning with somber gray. The air is heavy with soot and cinders; the smell is nauseating. In the distance, giant furnaces vomit pillars of fire, the lurid flames accentuating a line of frame structures, dilapidated and miserable. They are the homes of the workers who have created the industrial glory of Pittsburgh, reared its millionaires, its Carnegies and Fricks.

The sight fills me with hatred of the perverse social injustice that turns the needs of mankind into an Inferno of brutalizing toil. It robs man of his soul, drives the sunshine from his life, degrades him lower than the beasts, and between the milestones of divine bliss and hellish torture grinds flesh and blood into iron and steel, transmutes human lives into gold, gold, countless gold.

The great, noble People. But is it really great and noble to be slaves and remain content? No, no! They are awakening, awakening!

Contentedly the peaceful Monongahela stretches before me, its waters lazily rippling in the sunlight, and softly crooning to the murmur of the woods on the hazy shore. But the opposite bank presents a picture of sharp contrast. Near the edge of the river rises a high board fence, topped with barbed wire, the menacing aspect heightened by warlike watch-towers and ramparts. The sinister wall looks down on me with a thousand hollow eyes, whose evident murderous purpose fully justifies the name "Fort Frick." Groups of excited people crowd the open spaces between the river and the fort, filling the air with the confusion of many voices. Men carrying Winchesters are hurrying by, their faces grimy, eyes bold yet anxious. From the mill-yard gape the black mouths of the cannon, dismantled breastworks bar the passages, and the ground is strewn with burning cinders, empty shells, oil barrels, broken furnace stacks, and piles of steel and iron. The place looks like the aftermath of a sanguinary conflict—the symbol of our industrial life, of the ruthless struggle in which the *stronger*, the sturdy man of labor, is always the victim, because he acts *weakly*. But the charred hulks of the Pinkerton barges at the landing-place, and the blood-bespattered gangplank, bear mute witness that for once the battle went to the *really strong, to the victim who dared.*

[. . .] The door of Frick's private office, to the left of the reception-room, swings open as the colored attendant emerges, and I catch a flitting glimpse of the black-bearded, well-knit figure at a table in the back of the room.

"Mistah Frick is engaged. He can't see you now, sah," the negro says, handing back my card.

I take the pasteboard, return it to my case, and walk slowly out of the reception-room. But quickly retracing my steps, I pass through the gate separating the clerks from visitors, and, brushing the astounded attendant aside, I step into the office on the left, and I find myself facing Frick.

From an instant the sunlight, streaming through the windows, dazzles me. I discern two men at the further end of the long table.

"Fr-," I begin. The look of terror on his face strikes me as speechless. It is the dread of the conscious presence of death. "He understands," it flashes through my mind. With a quick motion I draw the revolver. As I raise the weapon, I see Frick clutch with both hands arm of the chair, and attempt to rise. I aim at his head. "Perhaps he wears armor," I reflect. With a look of horror he quickly averts his face, as I pull the trigger. There is a flash, and the high-ceilinged room reverberates as with the booming of cannon. I hear a sharp, piercing cry, and see Frick on his knees, his head against the arm of the chair. I feel calm and possessed, intent upon the movement of the man. He is lying head and shoulders under the large armchair, without sound or motion. "Dead?" I wonder. I must make sure. About twenty-five feet separate us. I take a few steps toward him, when suddenly the other man, whose presence I had quite forgotten, leaps upon me. I struggle to loosen his hold. He looks slender and small. I would not hurt him: I have no business with him. Suddenly I heard his cry, "Murder! Help!" My heart stands still as I realize that it is Frick shouting. "Alive?" I wonder. I hurl the stranger aside and fire at the crawling figure of Frick. The man struck my hand—I have missed! He grappled with me, and we wrestle across the room. I try to throw him, but spying an opening between his arm and body, I thrust the revolver against his side and aim at Frick, cowering behind the chair. I pull the trigger. There is a click—but no explosion! By the throat I catch the stranger, still clinging to me, when suddenly something heavy strikes me on the back of the head. Sudden pains shoot through my eyes. I sink to the floor, vaguely conscious of the weapon slipping from my hands.

"Where is the hammer? Hit him, carpenter!" Confused voices ring in my ears. Painfully I strive to rise. The weight of many bodies pressing on me. Now—it's Frick's voice! Not dead? . . . I crawl in the direction of the sound, dragging the struggling men with me. I must get the dagger from my pocket—I have it! Repeatedly I strike with it at the legs of the man near the window. I hear Frick cry out in pain—there is much shouting and stamping—my arms are pulled and twisted, and I am lifted bodily from the floor.

Police, clerks, workmen in overalls, surround me. An officer pulls my head back by the hair, and my eyes meet Frick's. He stands in front of me, supported by several men. His face is ashen gray; the black beard is streaked with red, and blood is oozing from his neck. For an instant a strange feeling, as of shame, comes over me; but the next moment I am filled with anger at the sentiment, so unworthy of a revolutionist. With defiant hatred I look him full in the face.

"Mr. Frick, do you identify this man as your assailant?"

Frick nods weakly.

The street is lined with a dense, excited crowd. A young man in civilian dress, who is accompanying the police, inquires, not unkindly:

"Are you hurt? You're bleeding."

I pass my hand over my face. I feel no pain, but there is a peculiar sensation about my eyes.

"I've lost my glasses," I remark, involuntarily.

"You'll be damn lucky if you don't lose your head," an officer retorts.

Source: Alexander Berkman, *Prison Memoirs of an Anarchist* (New York, NY: Mother Earth Publishing Association, 1912), 1–35.

Excerpt from Emma Goldman's memoirs

*B*erkman's longtime partner and lover, Emma Goldman, published her own
memoirs (titled Living My Life*) in* 1931. *The book is equal parts autobiography and manifesto, detailing her political convictions and her revolutionary
activities. The following selection describes her part in Berkman's (whom she called
Sasha, a nickname for Alexander) attempt to assassinate Henry Clay Frick
in 1892.*

It was May 1892. News from Pittsburgh announced that trouble had
broken out between the Carnegie Steel Company and its employees
organized in the Amalgamated Association of Iron and Steel Workers. It
was one of the biggest and most efficient labour bodies of the country
consisting mostly of Americans, men of decision and grit, who would assert
their rights. The Carnegie Company, on the other hand, was a powerful
corporation, known as a hard master. It was particularly significant that
Andrew Carnegie, its president, had temporarily turned over the entire
management to the company's chairman, Henry Clay Frick, a man known
for his enmity to labour. Frick was also the owner of extensive coke-
fields, whose unions were prohibited and the workers were ruled with an
iron hand.

The high tariff on imported steel had greatly boomed the American
steel industry. The Carnegie Company has practically a monopoly of it and
enjoyed unprecedented prosperity. Its largest mills were in Homestead, near
Pittsburgh, where thousands of workers were employed, their tasks
requiring long training and high skill. Wages were arranged between the
company and the union, according to a sliding scale based on the prevailing
market price of steel products. The current agreement was about to expire,
and the workers presented a new wage schedule, calling for an increase
because of the higher market prices and enlarged output of the mills.

The philanthropic Andrew Carnegie conveniently retired to his castle in Scotland, and Frick took full charge of the situation. He declared that henceforth the sliding scale would be abolished. The company would make no more arrangements with the Amalgamated Association; it would itself determine the wages to be paid. In fact, he would not recognize the union at all. He would not treat the employees collectively, as before. He would close the mills and the men might consider themselves discharged. Thereafter they would have to apply for work individually, and the pay would be arranged with every worker separately. Frick curtly refused the peace advances of the workers' organization, declaring that there was "nothing to arbitrate." Presently, the mills were closed. "Not a strike, but a lockout," Frick announced. It was an open declaration of war.

[. . .] Labour throughout the country was aroused. The steel-workers declared that they were ready to take up the challenge of Frick; they would insist on their right to organize and to deal collectively with their employers. Their tone was manly, ringing with the spirit of their rebellious forebears of the Revolutionary War.

Far away from the scene of the impending struggle, in our little ice-cream parlour in the city of Worcester, we eagerly followed developments. To us it sounded the awakening of the American worker, the long-awaited day of his resurrection [. . .]

One afternoon a customer came in for an ice-cream while I was alone in the store. As I set down the dish before him, I caught the large headlines of his paper: "LATEST DEVELOPMENTS IN HOMESTEAD-FAMILIES OF STRIKERS EVICTED FROM COMPANY HOUSES-WOMEN IN CONFINEMENT CARRIED OUT INTO THE STREET BY SHERIFFS." I read over the man's shoulder Frick's dictum to the workers: he would rather see them dead than concede to their demands, and he threatened to import Pinkerton detectives. The brutal bluntness of the account, the inhumanity of Frick toward the evicted mother, inflamed my mind. Indignation swept my whole being. I heard the man at the table ask: "Are you sick, young lady? Can I do anything for you?" "Yes, you can leave me your paper," I blurted out. "You won't have to pay me for the ice-cream. But I must ask you to leave. I must close the store." The man looked at me as if I had gone crazy.

I locked up the store and ran full speed the three blocks to our little flat. It was Homestead, not Russia; I knew it now. We belonged in Homestead. The boys, resting for the evening shift, sat up as I rushed into the room, newspaper clutched in my hand. "What has happened, Emma? You look terrible!" I could not speak. I handed them the paper.

Sasha was first on his feet. "Homestead!" he exclaimed. "I must go to Homestead!" I flung my arms around him, crying out his name. I, too, would go. "We must go tonight," he said; "the great moment has come at last!" Being internationalists, he added, it mattered not to us where the blow was struck by the workers; we must be with them. We must bring them our great message and help them see that it was not only for the moment that they must strike, but for all time, for a free life, for anarchism. Russia had many heroic men and women, but who was there in America? Yes, we must go to Homestead, tonight!

I had never heard Sasha so eloquent. He seemed to have grown in stature. He looked strong and defiant, an inner light on his face making him beautiful, as he had never appeared to me before.

[. . .] A few days [later] the news was flashed across the country of the slaughter of steel-workers by Pinkertons. Frick had fortified the Homestead mills, built a high fence around them. Then, in the dead of night, a barge packed with strike-breakers, under the protection of heavily armed Pinkteron thugs, quietly stole up the Monongahela River. The steel-men had learned of Frick's move. They stationed themselves along the shore, determined to drive back Frick's hirelings. When the barge got within range, the Pinkertons had opened fire, without warning, killing a number of Homestead men on the shore, among them a little boy, and wounding scores of others.

The wanton murders aroused even the daily papers. Several came out in strong editorials, severely criticizing Frick. He had gone too far; he had added fuel to the fire in the labour ranks and would have himself to blame for any desperate acts that might come.

We were stunned [. . .] Intuitively each felt what was surging in the heart of the others. Sasha broke the silence. "Frick is the responsible factor in this crime," he said; "he must be made to stand the consequences." [. . .] A blow aimed at Frick would re-echo in the poorest hovel, would call the attention of the whole world to the real cause behind the Homestead struggle. It would also strike terror in the enemy's ranks and make them realize that the proletariat of America had its avengers.

[. . .] "I will kill Frick," Sasha said, "and of course I will be condemned to death. I will die proudly in the assurance that I gave my life for the people. But I will die by my own hand . . . Never will I permit our enemies to kill me."

[. . .] "I will go with you, Sasha," I cried; "I must go with you. I know that as a woman I can be of help. I could gain access to Frick easier than you. I would pave the way for your act. Besides, I simply must go with you. Do you understand, Sasha?"

We had a feverish work. Sasha's experiments took place at night when everybody was asleep. While Sasha worked, I kept watch. I lived in dread every moment for Sasha, for our friends in the flat, the children, and the rest of the tenants. What if anything should go wrong—but, then, did not the end justify the means? Our end was the sacred cause of the oppressed and the exploited people. It was for them that we were going to give our lives. What if a few should have to perish?—the many would be made free and could live in beauty and comfort. Yes, the end in this case justified the means.

After we had paid our fare from Worcester to New York, we had about sixty dollars left [. . .] The material Sasha bought for the bomb had cost a good deal and we had another week in New York. Besides, I needed a dress and shoes which, together with the fare to Pittsburgh, would amount to fifty dollars. I realized with a start that we required a large sum of money. I knew no one who could give us so much; besides, I would never tell him the purpose. After days of canvassing in the scorching July heat I succeeded in collecting twenty-five dollars. Sasha finished his preparatory work and went to Staten Island to test the bomb. When he returned, I could tell by his expression that something terrible had happened. I learned soon enough; the bomb had not gone off.

Sasha said it was due either to the wrong chemical directions or to the dampness of the dynamite. The second bomb, having been made from the same material, would most likely also fail. A week's work and anxiety and forty precious dollars wasted! What now? We had no time for lamentations or regrets; we had to act quickly!

[. . .] Our whole fortune consisted of fifteen dollars. That would take Sasha to Pittsburgh, buy some necessaries, and still leave him a dollar for the first day's food and lodging. Our Allegheny comrades Nold and Bauer, whom Sasha meant to look up, would give him hospitality for a few days until I could raise more money. Sasha had decided not to confide his mission to them; there was no need for it, he felt, and it was never advisable for too many people to be taken into conspiratorial plans [. . .]

[. . .] Those with whom we were staying were told that Sasha would leave that evening, but the motive for his departure was not revealed. There was a simple farewell supper, everyone joked and laughed, and I joined the gaiety. I strove to be jolly to cheer Sasha, but it was laughter that masked suppressed sobs. Later we accompanied Sasha to the Baltimore and Ohio Station. Our friends kept in the distance while Sasha and I paced the platform, our hearts too full for speech.

The conductor drawled out: "All aboard!" I clung to Sasha. He was on the train, while I stood on the lower step. His face bent low to mine, his hand holding me, he whispered: "My sailor girl," (his pet name for me), "comrade, you will be with me to the last. You will proclaim that I gave what was dearest to me for an ideal, for the great suffering people."

The train moved. Sasha loosened my hold, gently helping me to jump off the step. I ran after the vanishing train, waving and calling to him:

"Sasha, Sashenka!" The steaming monster disappeared round the bend and I stood glued, straining after it, my arms outstretched for the precious life that was being snatched away from me.

[. . .] In the early afternoon of Saturday, July 23, Fedya rushed into my room with a newspaper. There it was, in large black letters: "YOUNG MAN BY THE NAME OF ALEXANDER BERKMAN SHOOTS FRICK—ASSASSIN OVERPOWERED BY WORKING-MEN AFTER DESPERATE STRUGGLE."

Working-men, working-men overpowering Sasha? The paper was lying! He did the act for the working-men; they would never attack him.

Hurriedly we secured the afternoon editions. Everyone had a different description, but the main fact stood out—our brave Sasha had committed the act! Frick was still alive, but his wounds were considered fatal. He would probably not survive the night. And Sasha—they would kill him. They were going to kill him, I was sure of it. Was I going to let him die alone? Should I go on talking while he was being butchered? I must pay the same price as he—I must stand the consequences—I must share the responsibility!

[. . .] [The following day] we read the detailed story about the "assassin Alexander Berkman." He had forced his way into Frick's private office on the heels of a Negro porter who had taken in his card. He had immediately opened fire, and Frick had fallen to the ground with three bullets in his body. The first to come to his aid, the paper said, was his assistant Leishman, who was in the office at the time. Working-men, engaged in a carpenter job in the building, rushed in, and one of them felled Berkman to the ground with a hammer. At first they thought Frick dead. Then a cry was heard from him. Berkman had crawled over and got near enough to strike Frick with the dagger in the thigh. After that he was pounded into unconsciousness. He came to in the station-house, he would answer no questions. One of the detectives grew suspicious of the appearance of Berkman's face and he nearly broke the young man's jaw trying to open his mouth. A peculiar capsule was found hidden there. When asked what it was, Berkman replied with defiant contempt: "Candy." On examination it proved to be a dynamite cartridge. The police were sure of a conspiracy. They were now looking for the accomplices, especially for a certain Bakhmetov, who had registered at one of the Pittsburgh hotels.

I felt that, on the whole, the newspaper accounts were accurate. Sasha had taken a poisoned dagger with him. "In case the revolver, like the bomb, fails to work," he had said. Yes, the dagger was poisoned—nothing could save Frick. I was certain that the papers lied when they said that Sasha had fired at Leishman. I remembered how determined he was that no one except Frick should suffer, and I could not believe that the working-men would come to the assistance of Frick, their enemy.

[. . .] Meanwhile the daily press carried on a ferocious campaign against the anarchists. They called for the police to act, to round up the "instigators, Johann Most, Emma Goldman, and their ilk." My name had rarely before been mentioned in the papers, but now it appeared every day in the most sensational stories. The police got busy; a hunt for Emma Goldman began.

My friend Peppie, with whom I was living, had a flat on Fifth Street and First Avenue, round the corner from the police station. I used to pass the latter frequently, going about openly and spending considerable time at the headquarters of the *Autonomie*. Yet the police seemed unable to find me. One evening, while we were away at a meeting, the police, having discovered my whereabouts at last, broke into the flat through the fire-escape and stole everything they could lay their hands on. My fine collection of revolutionary pamphlets and photographs, my entire correspondence, vanished with them. But they did not find what they were looking for. At the first mention of my name in the papers I had disposed of the material left over from Sasha's experiments. Since the police found nothing incriminating, they went after Peppie's servant, but she was too terrorized by the very sight of an officer to give them information. She stoutly denied that she had ever seen any man in the flat who looked like the photograph of Sasha which the detective had shown her.

Two days after the raid the landlord ordered us out of the flat. This was followed by a more serious blow—Mollock, Peppie's husband, who was working on Long Island, was kidnapped and spirited away to Pittsburgh, charged with complicity in Sasha's act.

Several days after the *Attentat* militia regiments were marched into Homestead. The more conscious of the steel-workers opposed the move, but they were overruled by the conservative labour element, who foolishly saw in the soldiers protection against new attacks by Pinkertons. The troops soon proved whom they came to protect. It was the Carnegie mills, not the Homestead workers.

However, there was one militiaman who was wide awake enough to see in Sasha the avenger of labour's wrongs. This brave boy gave vent to his feelings by calling for "three cheers for the man who shot Frick." He was court-martialled and strung up by his thumbs, but he stuck to his cheers. This incident was the one bright moment in the black and harrowing days that followed Sasha's departure.

After a long, anxious wait a letter came from Sasha. He had been greatly cheered by the stand of the militiaman, W. L. Iams, he wrote. It showed that even American soldiers were waking up. Could I get in touch with the boy, send him anarchist literature? He would be a valuable asset to the movement. I was not to worry about himself; he was in fine spirits and already preparing his court speech—not as defence, he emphasized, but in explanation of his act. Of course, he would have no lawyer; he would represent his own case as true Russians and other revolutionaries did. Prominent Pittsburgh attorneys had offered their services free of charge, but he had declined. It was inconsistent for anarchists to employ lawyers; I should make his attitude on the matter clear to his comrades [. . .]

[. . .] I pressed the letter to my heart, covering it with kisses. I knew how intensely my Sasha felt, although he had said not one word about his love and his thoughts of me.

Source: Emma Goldman, *Living My Life, Vol. II* (New York, NY: Cosimo Books, 2008), 83–100.

Senator John M. Palmer's Speech on Homestead

John M. Palmer was an Illinois politician, serving as the state's governor (1869–1873) and one of its senators (1891–1897). Palmer shifted political parties many times, moving from a Democrat in his youth to various shades of Republican during and after the Civil War before finally returning to the Democratic Party in the 1890s. Reminiscing about his long career, Palmer noted, "I had my own views. I was not a slave of any party." Palmer delivered the speech below on the floor of the U.S. Senate on July 7, 1892, and later included it in his posthumously published memoir.

"Mr. President, I did not understand the proposition of the senator from Maine until this moment. I now understand the purpose of the reference is to supply the means for the investigation of the circumstances of the affair at Homestead. I beg to say that the suggestion, therefore, is in line of the purpose I have in view. But, before the subject passes from the attention of the senate, I beg to make a few observations."

"I am quite satisfied that merely to deplore this condition of things falls very short of what must be the duty of some department or departments of either the state or federal governments. We are confronted now with this labor problem in its most impressive form."

"The very large establishment of the Carnegie Company, which, I understand, has some $25,000,000 capital behind it, or invested in its enterprise, employs some five thousand men, I believe, and upon these five thousand men there are dependent many thousand women and children who depend upon the proceeds of the labor of these men for support. I understand that the Carnegie Company have determined that there shall be changes in their methods; that there shall be a different rate of compensation hereafter paid for certain kinds of labor, and that the contracts shall end at another time of year, and that they shall make those conditions preemptory and absolute—the reductions of wages and the difference in the termination of the period of those contracts. It is also true that they have, in the exercise of what they claim to be their clear right, attempted to bring a large military force to their establishment—a military force which has a known and recognized existence in this country. The army raised and commanded by the Pinkertons is as distinctly known in this country as is the regular army of the United States. It is not a new thing; I am astonished to find that it excites surprise now. For years that force has existed; its number not always the same. The commander-in-chief of this army, like the barons of the middle ages, has a force to be increased at pleasure for the service of those who will pay him or them, and they have been employed in many states of the Union. They have been employed in New York, and have shed the blood of citizens of that state. They have been employed in Illinois, and have shed the blood of citizens of Illinois. At other points in the United States, they have been employed. This company claim not only the right to regulate their own business in their own way, but they claim the right to fortify their positions and the right to introduce this armed force within their fortified lines. They claim a right to a free passage from their armed boats on the Monongahela river into their fortifications; and hence, this struggle, this battle, because battles are not necessarily conflicts between armed men organized by proper authority, and there was a battle between the men who supposed they had a right and this armed force of mercenaries raised and organized by the owners of this establishment."

"Mr. President, in making this statement, I confess that I have given no information to the senate. We know what the facts are. It is claimed that the citizens fired on the mercenaries, and it is claimed on the other hand that the mercenaries fired first upon the citizens. It is not very much material, to my mind, who fired the first shot."

"These are men who were taken there for the purpose of battle, a contingent purpose, I confess, but for the purpose of shedding the blood of these people if they stood in their pathway."

"But even when that statement is made I have done but little towards reaching a solution of this question. What I desire from any committee of the senate will be not to tell us the story of this outrage, nor is it material whether the blame for the present condition is cast upon the Carnegie Company or not. It is simply because they are representatives of new conditions of society. It might have happened at any one of a hundred places in the United States where large numbers of men are employed in the service of these enormous manufacturing establishments. It may happen anywhere. It may occur in Illinois, or in New York, or in Pennsylvania, or Ohio. Anywhere it may happen, because in the nature of things these interests oppose each other up to the extent that I shall describe."

"I speak of the Carnegie Company merely because it happens to be an actor in these things. It is claimed for them, and by them, that they have an absolute right to the management of their own property; that they are not bound to listen to the suggestions or the wishes of any third person, that the men who have toiled with them for years have no voice whatever, have no interest in the establishment, have no right, and only speak by permission of those who employ them. That is the broad statement of property rights in the Carnegie Company."

"The men, who resist, claim that they have some rights, because it is true as a matter of law, and if it is to be regarded as true in a political sense, that these 4,500 men were simply trespassers there, then of course it must be very difficult to condemn the Carnegie Company, except as to the manner in which they assert their rights. It may be said that it was menacing and insulting that they should organize this force in contempt of public authority, because for a private citizen to attempt to enforce his own rights, however clear they may be, in disregard of the agents of the law, is contempt of the law; and this attempt to maintain their rights by the aid of an organized force was contempt of the State of Pennsylvania. The manner was menacing and insulting. To advance upon a peaceful, quiet city in the manner I have described was an insult to the people who were there."

"Mr. President, it is difficult for American citizens, whether they are in the right or wrong, to submit to be driven by an armed force. I confess that every impulse of my mind tempts me to feel that I should dislike being driven, even though I might be in the wrong, by a person who might happen to be in the right."

"I will not discuss that question. Something more, however, must be claimed for these men. I maintain—and I ask the attention of the committee on education and labor, if that committee shall be instructed to inquire into this matter—that these citizens were right. I maintain, according to the law of the land—not as the law is generally understood, but according to the principles of the law which must hereafter be applied to the solution of these troubles—that these men had a right to be there. That makes it necessary for me to assert that these men had a right to employment there, they had earned the right to live there, and these large manufacturing establishments—and there is no other road out of this question—must hereafter be understood to be public establishments in the modified sense which I will explain in a moment, in which the public is deeply interested, and the owners of these properties must hereafter be regarded as holding their property subject to the correlative rights of those without whose services the property would be utterly valueless. That concession which I make only concedes to them a right to a reasonable profit on the capital invested in their enterprises. I maintain, furthermore, that these laborers, having been in that service, having been engaged there, having spent their lives in this peculiar line of service, have a right to insist upon the permanency of their employment, and they have a right, too, to insist upon reasonable compensation for their services."

"We talk about the civil service law as applicable to government employment. I assert that there is a law wider and broader than that which gives to these men who have been bred in these special pursuits, as, for example, in the service of railroads, or of those vast manufacturing establishments, a right to demand employment, a right which can only be defeated by misconduct on their part."

"I maintain, therefore, that at the time of the assault upon these people at Homestead, they were where they had a right to be; they were upon ground they had a right to defend. Do you ask me if these men may by force take possession of the property of others? No. They were conducting themselves in the line of their rights as I understand them. Business was suspended and these men were simply awaiting the settlement of the disputed questions between themselves and their employers. Mark me. I maintain the right of owners of property to operate it at their will; I maintain the right of operatives to assist in its operation; I maintain the right of both parties to reasonable compensation for their services; I maintain the right of those laborers to continuous employment, dependent not alone upon the will of their employers, but dependent upon the good conduct of the employees."

"Mr. President—this is the only road out of the difficulty. You may call out the militia of the State of Pennsylvania, and you may exterminate all of the inhabitants of that beautiful and thrifty village, and what is done? Human life has again been sacrificed in one of those struggles for human rights. Do you establish the right of these large establishments to control their business? On the contrary, the laboring men of the country, so conscious of this right which I assert, the right to continue in employment during good behavior, will continue to resist, and this social war will be upon you and it becomes the duty of Christian statesmen, Republican statesmen, to find some road out of this difficulty. Within my lifetime I have seen marvelous changes. There was a time when individualism was the universal rule and men lived alone because they could support themselves; but matters have changed. To-day the world is practically divided between the employers and the employees. I do not take into account those neglected agricultural districts, those farm laborers for whom nobody seems to care, for in all the discussions of tariff policy we have had, nobody ever speaks of the toiler upon the farm. We speak of organized labor, and skilled labor, but when we come to talk about the white or the black men who toil upon the farm from the rising of the sun until the going down thereof, and speak of the influence of legislation upon these men, we do not regard them. If we pray for them, we pray for them very much the same as Brougham said the Queen was prayed for, for the desolate and the oppressed; if we legislate, they are not regarded. But this organized labor is power in the state. You must regard it; you must adjust their interests."

"How can you adjust it? You cannot do it by asserting, which I admit to be true, that every man has a right to control of his own property in his own way; or, if a man does not like to go to work for the Carnegies, he may go to work for somebody else. You cannot settle it by saying that Mr. Carnegie has a right to employ whomever he pleases. These are old truisms which have no application in this changed condition, when organized capital furnishes all that we have; it furnishes us our food; it furnishes all our clothing; it furnishes our physicians; I believe now it is furnishing our lawyers; and it is said that it has furnished us our legislators sometimes, although that is a slander which I am not disposed to indorse."

"That being the case, you have got to find some way out. You cannot admit the absolute right of capital; you cannot admit the absolute right of labor; you have to adjust their rights upon some basis. What is it?"

"That a manufacturing establishment is a public institution, as the railroads are held to be public, because they work for the public; public, because they employ the public, public because men employed in their service become unfit for other services, and public, because there are thousands dependent upon them for food and nurture."

"Thus we have recognized the right of the capitalist to control his property, and his right to a reasonable reward for his investment, and we claim for the laborer the right to permanent employment during good behavior, though he is certainly compelled to submit to the changes of business. Where the profits are small, the parties must divide the loss; where the profits are large, the profits must be divided."

"That is the exact condition; that is the law to-day, as I maintain, because the law is the perfection of reason, and we have seen the law built up step after step. I recollect, in 1869, I was compelled to hold that the legislature of Illinois had no right to arbitrarily fix the rates of carriage of passengers by railways, and was compelled to hold that the railway companies had no arbitrary right to fix them, but that was a matter of reasonableness on both sides. It was then claimed by the railroad corporations that their rights were absolutely uncontrollable. The same principle must now be applied to the solution of these troubles. These parties are now confronted on the banks of the Monongahela river. Whether the battle is going on to-day or not I do not know, but we have heard the report that the lives of American citizens have been lost in the battle. It will go on. I invoke this committee; I invoke this senate, if it shall appoint the committee at all, to let the committee have such powers as will allow them to look into the very heart of this question. It is a reproach to our civilization that this senate and country—perhaps the senate has no control over it beyond investigation—stand here now witnessing these two armed forces in battle array, and we confess we have no power except to inquire. Why inquire? What is the use of asking the bloody story be recited if there is nothing to be done? If this war is to go on forever, why meddle with it? Let it be solved as it may, you must find some principle by which this thing can be done."

"You cannot ask these laborers to become slaves, because if it is true, as claimed by some, that capitalists have a right to hold over the heads of their employees threats of dismissal at their pleasure, American freedom is gone, and the vote will be cast by the master who holds the bread of the slave. You must give to the voter, if you mean that he shall be independent, a fixity of employment, so that he may defy the employer, and say to him: 'My tenure depends, not on my vote, but my tenure depends upon my good behavior, upon my fidelity, my honesty, my industry and not upon my vote.' If some solution is not found in that direction, this army of employees will be controlled by the employers, and there will be established an aristocracy more terrible than exists in any free country, and this nobility of wealth will become our governors."

"But I may be asked: Shall these men lose their property? By no means. They shall hold their property subject to this public obligation, and in that alone we shall find the solution of this labor trouble. Capital and labor are confronting each other now. What is the condition? The employer attempts to control his property by force. Why is that so? Because American governments, federal and state, have neglected their duty. We have stood upon this volcano, and now we perceive the eruption, and it will occur constantly. These men are holding their position, as I maintain, rightfully, because they have a right to employment on reasonable terms. What, then, is the fault of the government? The government has as yet furnished no agency by which their controversies can be adjusted, and until this is done, this blood is on the hands of every government, state and federal, until they have exhausted all of the resources of reason and experience in finding some mode of avoiding these troubles. We may talk about the effect of these labor troubles politically. I find myself quoted, Mr. President, as having spoken of the influence of these troubles upon the presidential election. If I said anything on that subject to the reporter who interviewed me, I confess it was an utterance that ought not to have been made, for when we stand in the presence of these perils—for they are perils, and the firing on this boat may be the beginning of a civil conflict, we cannot tell—I say, to speak of their effect upon the near approaching election, is little short of a crime. I hope the committee on education and labor, if the resolution goes to that committee, will feel that when they furnish the senate with a history of this transaction they have performed a work of supererogation. They ought to furnish the senate with some principle or rule by which these controversies can be settled; because, if there is no rule of reason which can be applied to their solution, then they must be fought out. Either capital will be the master, and the people slaves, or the people of the country will be involved in anarchy, and capital destroyed."

"It cannot be in this country that, with the reason, the patriotism, the Christianity and intelligence which characterize our people, we shall fail to find some solution of this trouble. I have indicated the only road out of the difficulty which has yet occurred to me."

John M. Palmer, *Personal Recollections of John M. Palmer: The Story of An Earnest Life* (Cincinnati, OH: The Robert Clarke Company, 1901).

Bibliography

Beatty, Jack. *Age of Betrayal: The Triumph of Money in America, 1865–1900.* New York, NY: Alfred A. Knopf, 2007.

Bemis, Edward W. "The Homestead Strike," *The Journal of Political Economy 2,* no. 3 (June, 1894: 369–396.

Berkman, Alexander. *Prisons Memoirs of an Anarchist.* New York, NY: Mother Earth Publishing Association, 1912.

Berkman, Alexander. *Prison Memoirs of an Anarchist.* Ed. John William Ward. New York, NY: New York Review of Books, 1999.

Brands, H. W. *The Reckless Decade: America in the 1890s.* Chicago, IL: University of Chicago Press, 2002.

Bridge, James Howard. *A Romance of Millions: The Inside History of the Carnegie Steel Company.* New York, NY: The Aldine Book Company, 1903.

Bridges, Hal. "The Robber Baron Concept in American History." *Business History Review* 32, no. 1 (Spring 1958): 1–13.

Brody, David. *Steelworkers in America: The Nonunion Era.* New York, NY: Harper Torchbooks, 1960.

Burgoyne, Arthur G. *The Homestead Strike of 1892.* Pittsburgh, PA: University of Pittsburgh Press, 1979.

Byington, Margaret F. *Homestead: The Households of a Mill Town.* Pittsburgh, PA: University of Pittsburgh Press, 1974.

Carnegie, Andrew. *Triumphant Democracy: Or Fifty Years' March of the Republic.* New York, NY: Charles Scribner's Sons, 1887.

Carnegie, Andrew. "The Homestead Strike," *Autobiography of Andrew Carnegie.* New York, NY: Houghton Mifflin Company, 1920.

Carnegie, Andrew. *The Andrew Carnegie Reader.* Ed. John Frazier Wall. Pittsburgh, PA: University of Pittsburgh Press, 1992.

Cohen, Steven R. "Steelworkers Rethink the Homestead Strike of 1892." *Pennsylvania History* 48, no. 2 (April 1981): 155–177.

Demarest, Jr., David P. *"The River Ran Red": Homestead, 1892.* Pittsburgh, PA: University of Pittsburgh Press, 1992.

Dray, Philip. *There is Power in a Union: The Epic Story of Labor in America.* New York, NY: Doubleday, 2010.

Dubofsky, Melvyn. *The State and Labor in Modern America*. Chapel Hill, NC: University of North Carolina Press, 1994.

Dulles, Foster Rhea and Melvyn Dubofsky. *Labor in America*. Arlington Heights, IL: Harland Davidson, Inc., 1984.

Engerman, Stanley L., Ed. *Terms of Slavery: Slavery, Serfdom, and Free Labor*. Stanford, CA: Stanford University Press, 1999.

Foner, Philip S. *History of the Labor Movement in the United States, Volume I*. New York, NY: International Publishers Company, Inc., 1988.

Foner, Philip S. *History of the Labor Movement in the United States, Volume II*. New York, NY: International Publishers Company, Inc., 1988.

Garland, Hamlin. "Homestead and Its Perilous Trades: Impressions of a Visit," *McClure's Magazine* 3, no. 1 (June 1984).

Gillon, Steven M. *10 Days that Unexpectedly Changed America*. New York, NY: Three Rivers Press, 2006.

Gittelman, H. M. "Perspectives on American Industrial Violence." *Business History Review* 47, no. 1 (Spring 1973): 1–23.

Goldman, Emma. *Living My Life, Vol. II*. New York, NY: Cosimo Books, 2008.

Harvey, George. *Henry Clay Frick: The Man*. New York, NY: Charles Scribner's Sons, 1928.

Hessen, Robert. *Steel Titan: The Life of Charles M. Schwab*. New York, NY: Oxford University Press, 1975.

Higgens, John E. "Andrew Carnegie, Author." *Pennsylvania Magazine of History & Biography* 88, no. 4 (October 1964): 439–455.

Krass, Peter. *Carnegie*. Hoboken, NJ: John Wiley & Sons, Inc., 2002.

Krause, Paul. "Rethinking the Homestead Lockout on the Fourth of July." *Pittsburgh History* 75, no. 2 (Summer 1992): 53–109.

Krause, Paul. *The Battle for Homestead, 1880–1892: Politics, Culture, and Steel*. Pittsburgh, PA: University of Pittsburgh Press, 1992.

Kuritz, Hyman. "The Labor Injunction in Pennsylvania, 1891–1931." *Pennsylvania History* 29, no. 3 (July 1962): 306–321.

Lamont-Brown, Raymond. *Carnegie: "The Richest Man in the World."* Phoenix Mill, UK: Sutton Publishing, Ltd., 2005.

Livesay, Harold C. *Andrew Carnegie and the Rise of Big Business*. Glenview, IL: Scott, Foresman and Company, 1975.

Long, Priscilla. *Where the Sun Never Shines: A History of America's Bloody Coal Industry*. New York, NY: Paragon House, 1989.

Marcus, Irwin. "Change and Continuity: Steel Workers in Homestead, Pennsylvania, 1889–1895." *Pennsylvania Magazine of History and Biography* 111, no. 1 (January 1987): 61–75.

Marsha, John L. "Captain Fred, Co. I, and the Workers of Homestead." *Pennsylvania History* 46, no. 4 (October 1979): 291–311.

Misa, Thomas J. *A Nation of Steel: The Making of Modern American, 1865–1925*. Baltimore, MD: Johns Hopkins University Press, 1955.

Montgomery, David. *Beyond Equality: Labor and the Radical Republicans, 1862–1872*. New York, NY: Alfred A. Knopf, 1967.

Montgomery, David. "Strikes in Nineteenth-Century America." *Social Science History* 4, no. 1 (Winter 1980): 81–104.

Nasaw, David. *Andrew Carnegie*. New York, NY: The Penguin Press, 2006.

Nicholson, Philip Yale. *Labor's Story in the United States*. Philadelphia, PA: Temple University Press, 2004.

Oates, William C., George Tickner Curtis, and T. V. Powderly. "The Homestead Strike." *North American Review* 155, no. 430 (September 1892): 355–375.

Oliver, John W. "Henry Clay Frick, Pioneer-Patriot and Philanthropist, 1849–1919." *Western Pennsylvania Historical Magazine* 32, nos. 3 & 4 (September–December 1949): 67–78.

Palmer, John M. *Personal Recollections of John M. Palmer: The Story of An Earnest Life*. Cincinnati, OH: The Robert Clarke Company, 1901.

Rees, Jonathan. "Homestead in Context: Andrew Carnegie and the Decline of the Amalgamated Association of Iron and Steel Workers." *Pennsylvania History* 64, no. 4 (Autumn 1997): 509–533.

Robinson, Jesse Squibb. *The Amalgamated Association of Iron, Steel, and Tin Workers*. Baltimore, MD: The Johns Hopkins Press, 1920.

Rosenbloom, Joshua L. "Strikebreaking and the Labor Market in the United States, 1881–1894." *Journal of Economic History* 58, no. 1 (March 1998): 183–205.

Schreiner, Samuel A. *Henry Clary Frick: The Gospel of Greed*. New York, NY: St. Martin's Press, 1995.

Serrin, William. *Homestead: The Glory and Tragedy of an American Steel Town*. New York, NY: Times Books/Random House, 1992.

Skrabec, Jr., Quentin R. *The Boys of Braddock: Andrew Carnegie and the Men Who Changed Industrial History*. Westminster, MD: Heritage Books, 2004.

Skrabec, Jr., Quentin R. *Henry Clay Frick: The Life of the Perfect Capitalist*. Jefferson, NC: MacFarland & Company, Inc., 2010.

Smith, Robert Michael. *From Blackjacks to Briefcases: A History of Commercialized Strikebreaking and Unionbusting in the United States*. Athens, OH: Ohio University Press, 2003.

Standiford, Les. *Meet You in Hell: Andrew Carnegie, Henry Clay Frick, and the Bitter Partnership that Transformed America*. New York, NY: Crown Publishers, 2005.

Taft, Phillip. "Violence in American Labor Disputes." *Annals of the American Academy of Political and Social Science* 364 (March 1966): 127–140.

Tausig, F. W. "The Homestead Strike." *Economic Journal* 3, no. 10 (June 1893): 307–318.

Wall, John Frazier. *Andrew Carnegie*. Pittsburgh, PA: University of Pittsburgh Press, 1989.

Warren, Kenneth. "The Business Career of Henry Clay Frick." *Pittsburgh History* 73 (Spring 1990): 3–15.

Warren, Kenneth. *Triumphant Capitalism: Henry Clay Frick and the Industrial Transformation of America*. Pittsburgh, PA: University of Pittsburgh Press, 1996.

Winkler, John K. *Incredible Carnegie: The Life of Andrew Carnegie (1835–1919)*. Garden City, NY: Garden City Publishing Company, 1931.

Wolff, Leon. *Lockout: A Story of the Homestead Strike of 1892: The Study of Violence, Unionism, and the Carnegie Steel Empire*. New York, NY: Harper & Row, 1965.

Index